COLBERTIANS

A History of Colbert County, Alabama, and Some of Its Pioneer Citizens Before 1875.

R. L. JAMES

Originally Published 1945
The Alabama Historical Quarterly

Southern Historical Press, Inc.
Greenville, South Carolina

This volume was repropuced from
a personal copy located in the
Publisher's private library
Greenville, South Carolina

All rights reserved. No part of this publication may be reproduced, stored in a retieval system, Transmitted in any form, posted on to the web in any form or by any means without the prior permission of the publisher.

Please direct ALL correspondence and book orders to:
www.southernhistoricalpress.com
or
Southern Historical Press, Inc.
PO Box 1267
Greenville, SC 29602-1267
southernhistoricalpress@gmail.com

Originally published: Montgomery, AL   1945
ISBN #0-89308-878-1
All Rights Reserved
Printed in the United States of America

— TABLE OF CONTENTS —

Preface iii

Biography, Robert Leslie James v

Colbertians

    Section I.   Historical 159

    Section II. Special Score of Families 174

    Section III. Obituaries and Cemetery Records 369

    Section III. Continued 500

    Section IV. Words of Praise 504

Errata and Additions 599

Index to Places 601

Index to Cemeteries 605

Index to Names 607

PREFACE

Genealogists are constantly asking that scattered information be consolidated and that out-of-print information be reprinted. Colbertians, by R. L. James, has both attributes, and these were the reasons that the Natchez Trace Genealogical Society used for justifying this reprint. Colbertians was printed as a series of articles in The Alabama Historical Quarterly in 1945. Although this journal is available in many libraries in the United States, copies of the older issues no longer can be purchased. Thus, this reprint consolidates the articles under a single cover and makes Colbertians once again available to a new generation of genealogists.

A reprint would not have been possible without the cooperation and work of several individuals. Richard C. Sheridan, Corinne King Murphy, and the Florence-Lauderdale Public Library loaned copies of the Quarterly for photocopying by the printer. Milo B. Howard, Jr., Director of the Department of Archives and History for the State of Alabama, is the present editor of The Alabama Historical Quarterly. He unreservedly granted permission for the articles to be reprinted. The Board of Directors of the Natchez Trace Genealogical Society has consistently provided encouragement in the task of reprinting.

Three other individuals deserve a special commendation. Kitty (Mrs. Victor, Jr.) Futrell Cox agreed to index the places, cemeteries, and people named in the James articles. Genealogical indexing is a specialty in which there are no guidelines and few people are experienced. Mrs. Cox's indexes add greatly to the value of the reprint to genealogists. One of the attributes of the name index is the indexing of nicknames along with given names. Many times only the nickname survives in family traditions; inclusion of the nickname in the name index thus increases the value of the index to the researcher. Please note that the given name is placed in parentheses adjacent to the nickname and that there is no page reference for the nickname. The searcher who locates a person by nickname should follow through by using the page number(s) quoted for the given name. Still another attribute of the name index is the listing of the maiden name of a married lady when such was known. This surname is given in parentheses adjacent to the given name. A page reference(s) is given for this listing but the researcher also should check for additional page numbers for that given name in the regular alphabetical listing of the surname.

Margaret James Smithson prepared the biography of her cousin, Robert Leslie James. Although she described James as a loner, the term should not be interpreted too literally. James liked people; he just didn't want to have them around him all the time. He found as much pleasure in walking the woods and streams as he did in visiting with people. He had an excellant memory of plants, places, people, and events. Once, when Margaret James was a small child, R. L. James dropped in for a visit with the family; it was Margaret's birthday. Years later, Mr. James recalled in detail the menu of the birthday lunch; the poke salad and molasses pudding stood at the head of the list because they were his favorite dishes.

Corinne King Murphy graciously volunteered to review James' articles for errors. James had depended upon personal interviews, old newspapers, letters, and census records for his information. Mrs. Murphy relied upon her extensive work with the primary records in Northwest Alabama and her intimate knowledge of Colbert County family relationships while reviewing James' work. As can be seen on page 599, James was a careful worker. His errors were few. Mrs. Murphy made her changes and additions on the basis of the information available to her. Additional discoveries in future years could require still more corrections and additions; hence there can be no assuarance that the information here presented about the early settlers of Colbert Co. is faultless.

One final comment about this reprint. We chose to make no corrections or changes in the articles as they were printed in the Quarterly. Even the page numbers are retained, and these are the ones used in the three indexes. Pages 159-222 appeared in Volume 7, No. 2, Summer Issue, 1945, of The Alabama Historical Quarterly. Pages 369-400 were in Volume 7, No. 3, Fall Issue, 1945; and pages 500-536 were in Volume 7, No. 4, Winter Issue, 1945. All other pages have been prepared by members of the Natchez Trace Genealogical Society.

Darrell A. Russel
Publications Chairperson
Natchez Trace Genealogical Society

ROBERT LESLIE JAMES

Robert Leslie James was born 2 March 1897 in a log house about five miles northwest of Russellville, Franklin Co., AL. He was the youngest of four sons born to Aaron A. and Ollie Virginia (Bendall) James. The house, which has been restored, still stands in the curve of a narrow country road. This house also was the birthplace of Ollie Virginia Bendall, mother of the four boys.

Aaron A. James was the son of Thomas and Elizabeth James who came to Franklin Co. from Bedford Co., TN. Thomas was Irish, a member of the Baptist Church, a Mason, and a Democrat. He owned a plantation of 700 acres on Duncan Creek in Franklin Co. and used slaves to do the farming.

Ollie Virginia Bendall was the daughter of Benjamin Franklin and Matilda Bendall. The Bendalls were early settlers in Franklin Co., coming from Virginia. They owned the log house before selling it to Aaron James and his wife. The house was built prior to 1827 according to family records.

R. L. James attended elementary school in Franklin Co. and graduated from the Russellville High School. He enlisted in the U. S. Army on 4 September 1918 and was honorably discharged on 1 January 1919. He qualified for a teacher's certificate and taught at several different schools in Franklin Co. Some of these schools were Fairview, Frankfort, Jonesboro, and Union Hill. He attended Florence State Teachers College, Florence, AL, and graduated in 1929. He also took some botany courses by correspondence from The University of Tennessee.

James was a loner. His interests were reading, writing short stories, history, and botany. Although he occasionally dated another teacher, he never married. He lived at home with his parents when not teaching school. After the deaths of his father and mother, he lived for a while in their home. In January 1949, however, he moved to Mountain Home, TN (near Johnson City), a home for retired soldiers. There he remained until his death at the Veterans Administration Hospital there on 23 January 1977. He was buried in the National Veterans Cemetery near Johnson City, TN.

James was the author of several articles in botanical magazines. He had a plant genus named after him, _Jamesianthus Alabamesis_, a perennial wildflower with yellow blossoms that grows on the banks of small streams in Colbert and Franklin Co. Prior to the series of articles on the early settlers of Colbert Co., James had privately published a history of about 120 Franklin Co. families. This book was published in 1930 as "Distinguished Men, Women and Families of Franklin County".

COLBERTIANS

By R. L. James, Russellville, Ala.

(There is a continual growing interest in local history throughout the country. The article "Colbertians", painstakingly prepared by Mr. James gives an intimate picture of the early history of Colbert County and some of its pioneer citizens. The next issue of the Quarterly will carry another article by Mr. James giving the same kind of early history of Franklin County. The writer, Robert Leslie James, of Russellville, was born March 2, 1897 near Russellville, in Franklin County, the son of Aaron A. and Ollie Virginia (Bendall) James, also of Franklin County. He attended the Florence State Teachers College from which he graduated in 1929 after which he taught school at several points. In addition to delving into the earliest history of his County he is a distinguished botanist and has written magazine articles on botanical subjects. He has a plant genus named for him, Jamesianthus, one of the few men in the State to be thus honored.)

PREFACE

I have no apology to offer for attempting to write *Colbertians*. I hope that the article will prove interesting to the citizens of Colbert County and also to many others scattered over the country. I have taken great pains to present the truth. Imagination is a great thing to have and the writer of Poetry must have it, but the writer of history, biography, or genealogy should never substitute imagination for truth even if the truth at times is prosaic. I have tried to make every sentence in *Colbertians* a truthful sentence. A large percent of this article is quoted. But I believe the ones quoted were honest and therefore their statements can be relied on.

At this time I am releasing two "sections" of Colbertians. I hope to have the privilege of adding at least one more section in the near future. There are many characters who should have recognition that are not included in the present two sections.

Practically no notice is taken of a number of very distinguished persons such as Gov. Lindsay and Col. W. A. Johnson. But I feel that they are so well known through the writings of various Alabama historians that I can well devote the space to other characters.

However, I want it understood that the amount of space devoted to any individual or family does not indicate the relative importance of that individual or family. Much more data can be obtained on certain individuals and families than others. For example, the space devoted to the O. H. Perry Williams family is small compared to that devoted to the James W. Ligon family. But as far as I know the Williams family was as important as the Ligon family.

The year 1875 is the "dead-line" for *Colbertians*. As a rule all characters treated in this article were born before 1875 and all events mentioned occurred before 1875.

The term "the war" as used throughout the article refers to the Civil War, or if you prefer, to the War Between the States or the War of Secession.

In listing the children of a family I have tried to list them according to age as near as I could ascertain but no claim is made to perfection in this matter. I am due thanks to so many different persons for data and other help that I fear I can not name near all of them. However I must acknowledge my appreciation to Mrs. Marie B. Owen, Director of State Department of Archives and History; John B. Sockwell, Probate Judge of Colbert and his office personnel; Mrs. Stanley, Circuit Clerk of Colbert; Paul Coburn, representative from Colbert; Miss Henderson, the Librarian of the Helen Keller Library at Tuscumbia; Miss Nina Leftwich, author of *"Two Hundred Years at Muscle Shoals"*; and to Hon. A. H. Carmichael, Miss Bessie Rather, Miss Mary Wallace Kirk, Mrs. Harriet McGregor, Mrs. Irene Leggett, Miss Julia Goodloe, Miss Julia Throckmorton, Mrs. Russey, Mrs. Finley, Mr. John Underwood, Mr. John Sherrod, Mr. Fletcher Bickley, Mrs. John Donley, Mr. A. F. Ricks, Miss Birdie Ricks, Mr. and Mrs. Wm. H. Sledge, Mrs. Ethel Ligon Sitton, Mr. and Mrs. T. B. Coburn, Mr. Henry Dotson, Hon. John D. Rather, Miss Mary McClain, Mrs. Emma Brown, Mrs. Lula Merrill Simpson, Mr. and Mrs. Will Clounch, and Mr. John Hobgood all who either live in Tuscumbia or live on rural routes radiating from Tuscumbia.

Mrs. Rush King, Mrs. James Smith, Mr. Woodruff Delony, Mr. F. W. McCormack and Mrs. J. W. Boatright, are among those at Leighton who gave me much valuable information and rendered valuable assistance.

Mrs. C. F. Turner and Mrs. Calvin Patterson and daughter,

Mrs. Knight, at Cherokee were very kind in assisting me to obtain information.

Among those who do not live in Colbert who furnished valuable information were Mr. and Mrs. W. C. Holesapple, Mrs. Emma Payne Alsobrook, and Miss Mima Scruggs of Florence; Mrs. H. W. Cranford Jasper; Mr. W. B. Kimbrough, Mr. and Mrs. R. L. McNatt, Mr. Geo. W. Quillin and Mr. Thomas Looney of Russellville; Mrs. Van A. Lester, Duncan, Miss.; Miss Frank Mahan, Meridian, Miss.; Mrs. John P. Ricks, Jackson, Miss. and her daughter, Mrs. Love of Yazoo City, Miss.; Mrs. Cleve Coats and Mrs. J. W. Atkins of Coal Hill, Ark. and Miss Birdie Srygley, Nashville, Tennessee.

Special thanks are due Mrs. B. W. Gandrud of Tuscaloosa, the former Miss Pauline Myra Jones of Huntsville, for very kind assistance in many ways. Mrs. Gandrud is the author of valuable historical works and is a genealogist of much consequence.

R. L. James

Russellville, Ala., January 31, 1946.

SECTION I—HISTORICAL

Colbert County, Alabama, is the only Colbert County in the United States of America, although I believe there was at one time a Colbert County in Mississippi. It is in the northwestern part of Alabama on the Mississippi border. It lies between 34 degrees and 35 degrees N. Lat. and is crossed by the 88th meridian W. Long. It has four counties bordering it. They are Lawrence on the east, Lauderdale on the north, Franklin on the south and Tishomingo, which is in Mississippi, on the west.

Colbert County was first established in 1867, the year of the Alaska Purchase. Its territory was taken from Franklin County which was created in February 1818. However Franklin County as originally established did not extend from the present Lawrence County to the Mississippi border. The western portion of what is now Franklin and Colbert Counties remained property of the Chickasaw Indians until 1832. Cane Creek, also spelled "Caney" Creek on old maps, was part of the border of the original Franklin County. This Creek crosses the Lee Highway and the Southern

Railroad about a mile or so east of Barton. Colbert County as originally created did not extend east to the stream called Town Creek. The road running north and south through Leighton was then the line between Colbert and Lawrence counties and had formerly been the line between Franklin and Lawrence Counties —hence it was, and is yet, called "*The County-Line Road.*" This road remained the line until the early part of 1895. In that year all the territory east of the County Line Road and west of the stream called Town Creek and extending north to the Tennessee River was taken from Lawrence and annexed to Colbert. This territory comes practically to a point at its southern end—the present southeast corner of Colbert County. It is not stretching the imagination a great deal to call this territory a triangle. Therefore, for convenience, I am going to refer to this part of Colbert County as the "*Town Creek-Triangle*".

The *Town Creek-Triangle* contains much excellent level land and attracted many men who were large planters or became large planters. Among them were Elisha Madding, Hartwell King, Manoah B. Hampton, Amos Jarman and Richard Prewit.

The year 1895 marked another change in the boundary lines of Colbert which I believe was the final one. Before then what is now Stout's Beat in Northeastern Franklin, or a large portion of it, was a part of Colbert. In that year that territory was returned to Franklin County. But before going further I should state that the Colbert County established in 1867, was abolished in November, 1867 and returned to Franklin and it was in Dec. 9, 1869, that the county had its "re-birth". Those were dark days in Alabama politics and a history of the abolishment and reestablishment of Colbert would take up too much space in an article such as I propose to write.

Now let us notice the Colberts for whom the county was named. I shall refer the reader to two sources of information that I have on the Colberts. First I shall quote from Leftwich's "*Two Hundred Years at Muscle Shoals*". The following appears on pages 19 and 20: "Prior to 1740, James Logan Colbert, a Scotch youth, lived in the Carolinas; later he joined the English traders traveling west and stopped at the Muscle Shoals. He married a Chickasaw wife and here was born George Colbert about 1764; William was an older brother; Levi and James were younger. At twenty six George built a comfortable residence on the south bank of the Tennessee River where the government's new Post route, famously known as the *Natchez Trace,* was to cross the river. A few miles southwest of his home lived his youngest brother, James Colbert, who shared well the honors of the family—he being the archivest and historian of the Chickasaw Nation. Levi, the incorruptible, lived at Buzzard Roost. William did not live in Colbert County, but at Pontotoc, the capital of the Nation. George later moved to that part of the Nation known as Tupelo and at the two plantations worked 140 slaves and became the wealthiest of the brothers. H. B. Cushman in his history refers to George Colbert as an exceedingly handsome man. The late James Simpson of Florence, said he was tall, slender and handsome, with long straight black hair, the features of an Indian, but lighter skin, very hospitable. Once he entertained for some time Jere Austill and his father Evan Austill when they were water bound on the *Natchez Trace.* He was courageous. It has been said that he fought with Jackson; a cut in one of the walnut columns of his porch being pointed out as having received the cut intended for the old general. Mr. King says such could not have been the case for had two men of the nature of those two fought, one would have been left on the spot. While he looked to his own interests, he did not forget those of his people. Old residents remember a speech delivered on the streets of Tuscumbia in 1832 in protest against the policy of the United States government in sending the Indians to the far West."

Mr. Paul Coburn has made a special study of the history of the Natchez Trace and of the Colberts. In request for some information on the Colberts Mr. Coburn very kindly wrote me a letter which I shall reproduce in full.

"Tuscumbia, Ala.

December 5, 1945

Mr. R. L. James
Russellville, Ala.

Dear Mr. James.

In answer to yours of Dec. 1 asking for some historical data concerning the Colbert Indians of this section I shall give you from memory as much information as I can.

"More history can be obtained from *Haywood's History of Tennessee* or the Mississippi Historical publications about the Colberts than from any Alabama history that I have ever been able to read. It is from each of the above mentioned copies that I will be able to give the following records and remember, it will be from memory as I don't have either of those books at present. Lochland Colbert, a Scotchman, deserted Braddock at Fort DuQuesne during the French and Indian war and wandered through the wilderness for quite some time finally coming into North Mississippi where he settled and married Sopha, an Indian Chief's daughter (whose name I can not recall). He was a Chickasaw of much consequence.

They reared five children. I can not recall one of their names, but William, Levi, George and Sopha all were very famous and outstanding. George and William were commissioned as Major Generals in the United States army during the Revolutionary war; Levi was Grand Council Chief of the Chickasaw Nation for many years up and down Big Bear Creek. Sopha married a white man and was the mother of several prominent early Mississippians.

"George Colbert for whom Colbert County was named lived at Georgetown about eight miles north of Cherokee, ran a ferry on the Old Natchez Trace and owned the entire west end of Colbert and Lauderdale Counties and eight hundred slaves and eight hundred ponies. It is said that he was known as one of the richest men of the entire Tennessee Valley.

"Before he left Alabama in 1835 he ran a large trading post or store at Georgetown; he was very honest and did a flourishing business. He hired a young man named Louis Alsobrook to work in his store. Alsobrook's father and mother died at Spring Valley. Bradley Alsobrook moved to a place now known as Alsoboro farther down on the Old Natchez Trace and named for the Alsobrooks.

"Chief Colbert was the father of two beautiful girls one of whom Louis Alsobrook was very much in love with. After the Indians left here in 1836 Alsobrook followed them to the Indian Territory still in pursuit of the girl's hand in matrimony. But to his disappointment she rejected him again so he prepared to come back to Alabama. He let the old Chief know that he thought he was the cause of the girl's decision; this seemed to have hurt the old Chief's feelings so as a token of good will he gave the young man a medal which President Thomas Jefferson gave him for the part he played in the war with England and the Creeks.

"Louis Alsobrook came back to Alabama, took down with slow fever and died. The medal is still in possession of the Bradley Alsobrook family. Another medal was found at Pontotoc, Miss. which had been presented to William Colbert at the same time, 1812. I am told that a contractor found it about six feet deep in earth as he excavated for a road in 1933 and he sold it to the Smithsonian Institute for a great price.

"Many other stories are told about the Colberts and their famous exploits. I am going to try to get that history from Mr. Frank King's daughter for you—*Haywood's History of Tenn.*—but they are very hard to find. The last publication was in 1821 (1921?) but it gives much valuable and rare information about the Tennessee Valley.

Very truly your Friend.

Paul Coburn".

Colbert County is a county of diverse contrasts in many ways. Roughly speaking the northern part is level and was originally very fertile. But of course there are small hills and places that were stony or not so fertile in the early days, much of the southern border and southwestern section is hilly or even mountainous. The entire drainage of the county goes to the Tennessee River which separates it from Lauderdale. There are many creeks and small streams in the county. Most of them have their sources within the county and flow directly into the river or into larger creeks. The largest of these is Big Bear Creek which flows through part of the western section. This stream rises in south eastern Franklin county, flows across the northwestern corner of Winston, on into Marion, back into Franklin, then into Tishomingo County, Mississippi, back into Alabama entering Colbert. The part of this creek that is in Colbert is now really a small river since Pickwick Dam in Tennessee has been built.

Among other streams of Colbert might be mentioned Buzzard Roost Creek and Rock Creek of the western section, each of these streams being tributaries of Big Bear; Cane Creek of historical interest since it (as I have already said) was part of the boundary between the original Franklin county and Chickasaw territory. Bear Creek (also called "Stinking Bear") with its tributaries of Ligon, Cook's, Mose Branch, Smith and Mill Creeks; Spring Creek with its tributaries of Fox-trap, Bull-Skull, and James; and Town Creek on the eastern border with Poplar and McAfee Creeks draining into it. It is interesting to note that of these named streams Cane Creek and its entire drainage system is within the confines of Colbert County. Among its tributaries are Henson Creek and Jackson Mill Creek. On one of the streams that make its headwaters is a waterfall said to be of much scenic interest. I have not as yet seen it. Between two other streams forming its headwaters as a bluff where the Mountain Laurel, or Ivy, grows so profusely that many years ago it was given the name of *"The Ivy Point"* I might as well say here that the native people of Colbert, at least a large proportion of them, did not call this beautiful native shrub Mountain Laurel but called it "Ivy". For the benefit of those readers who are critical and demand the scientific names of plants the shrub in question is *Kalmia Latifolia* named in honor of the botanist Peter Kalm a friend of Linnaeus. Perhaps the majority of the pioneers of Colbert had but little admiration for Ivy or Mountain Laurel regardless of its wondrous lovely flowers and evergreen foliage because it might kill their best milch cows if they ate of it. And a certain pioneer citizen of Colbert, deciding to commit suicide made a tea of its leaves and drank it. Bear Creek and Spring Creek have their sources in Franklin County, each within three miles of Russellville, and flow clear across Colbert. On Ligon Creek was the noted Ligon Springs and on Cook's Creek is a bluff of historical and scenic interest called *"Cook's Bluff"*. Fox-trap Creek, whose name suggests a hunter's or trapper's paradise in the early days is of much botanical interest. Bull Skull is said to have received its name from the fact that many years ago a wild and ferocious bull ranged about its headwaters, which is near the old Russellville and LaGrange Road. In those days that road was much traveled, many of the people using ox-teams. Some times the travelers camped in the region where the wild bull had his haunts and their oxen were terrified by him. At length some one shot him through the head and for a long while after his skull remained with the bullet hole through it—hence the name Bull-Skull Creek.

But Poplar Creek has a different kind of interest. I don't know why it was called Poplar Creek. At present there seems to be very few trees of that name along the creek but they may have been more abundant years ago. At present "Beech Creek" would be an appropriate name for there are quite a lot of beech trees there. But the historical interest of Poplar Creek is this: The First Steam Mill in North Alabama was on Poplar Creek about three miles southwest of old LaGrange. At least that was what Prof. John C. Stephenson, at one time a professor in LaGrange College wrote in the "Leighton News" some 35 or 40 years ago. Prof. Stephenson stated that the mill was the property of Josiah Horn and associated with him was a young bachelor from Tennessee-Daniel Spangler. This mill was a saw and grist mill combined. Prof. Stephenson said there was a large amount of Pine there and Horn's mill sawed the pine trees into lumber and ground the corn (and wheat, too, I suppose) for the settlers. He stated that young Spangler had full charge of the grist department and finally became owner of the mill. Later it was moved into Lawrence County. People came to see Horn's Mill on Poplar Creek in operation from as far as 20 miles away according to Prof. Stephenson. The steam mill on Poplar Creek was in operation in the 1830's. I shall probably have more to say about both Mr. Horn and Mr. Spangler further on.

But Colbert was not only the place of North Alabama's first steam mill. Within the present Colbert County was the First Chartered College in Alabama, the First Railroad in Alabama and one of the first in the United States, and a part of the First Postal Route in the South. Colbert also furnished the First and only Foreign Born Governor that Alabama has had, and a daughter of that governor became Alabama's greatest Kindergarten Teacher and one of the greatest in America as well as a distinguished author of children's stories. And of course there is Helen Keller, one of the world's marvels. To those who love birds I can say that F. W. McCormack, a native born and life long citizen of Leighton, is one of the most distinguished ornithologists of the South. He wrote a fine work on the birds of Colbert County before he had attained twenty years of age. Mr. McCormack published the "*Leighton News*" for many years which was a splendid local paper, and served the people of Leighton a number of years as Postmaster. He is now 72 years young and still "running in high"

His parents were born in Ireland but were married in America, and lived for many years in Leighton.

I could speak further of scenic places of interest in Colbert— a few of which are Sand Rock at LaGrange; Red Rock a few miles south or southeast of Barton; The Billy Sanderson Cave on the road between Barton and Frankfort; Newsom's Springs near Billy Sanderson Cove; Raven Bluff near Littleville; Colbert Heights on Jackson Highway south of Tuscumbia and many places along Lake Wilson and the Tennessee River—but I have perhaps already devoted too much space to this subject.

Among the old towns of Colbert were, Tuscumbia, Leighton, LaGrange, Bainbridge, South Florence, and York's Bluff. Leftmich's *"Two Hundred Years at Muscle Shoals"* discusses most of these places very interestingly. Bainbridge calls to my mind an interesting but sad occurance of the early days which was recorded by Col. J. E. Saunders in his *"Early Settlers of North Alabama"*. On page 197 of that work where he was discussing Major Dillahunty, the pioneer settler of Courtland, Alabama, may be found the following paragraph:

"Major Dillahunty lived three years at Courtland, and then moved to the neighborhood of Mount Pleasant Church. He purchased lands for his father, Thomas Dillahunty and for his father-in-law, John Johnson. When his father died in 1829 his place was sold to Vincler Jones, and Mr. Johnson's place was the one now occupied by Stewart Hennigan. While Major Dillahunty lived at Mt. Pleasant occurred the first Masonic burial that ever took place in the county, and Major Dillahunty, who was then the highest mason performed the ceremony. It was that of Jack Ethridge. He had been married one day to Martha Beavers, and the next day he rode to Bainbridge with a friend, and on returning they concluded to try the speed of their horses, and Ethridge was thrown against a tree and killed. I judge she earlier became a widow than any wife ever in our county."

Mount Pleasant at the time of the above incident was in Lawrence County, but that neighborhood is now in the Town Creek-Triangle.

The states of North Carolina, Tennessee, Virginia, South

Carolina, Kentucky and Georgia was the birthplace of the majority of the first settlers of Colbert County—perhaps about in the order named. It appears that North Carolina held first place and Tennessee second. Many families from Virginia and the Carolinas settled first in Tennessee then removed to Alabama. It so happened that in the same family some of the children were perhaps born in Virginia, some in Tennessee and some in Alabama. For example two very outstanding lawyers and citizens of Tuscumbia for many years before the War and for a long time after, were William Cooper and Lydal Cooper. They were brothers but William was a Virginian by birth and Lydal a Tennessean. Then there were the Winstons. Anthony Winston, a Revolutionary soldier, was of a prominent Virginia family having been born in Hanover County, but "emigrated to Tenn. at an early period" and later came to Colbert County (then Franklin) and died here in 1827 or 1828. I believe most or all of his sons who settled about Tuscumbia were born in Tennessee.

It appears without a doubt that no other state was the birthplace of so many men distinguished more or less for wealth in Colbert as North Carolina. That state was the birthplace of John G. Shine, F. W. Bynum, Drury Vinson, Abraham Ricks, Isaac Lane, Hartwell King, Oswald King, Robert King, J. C. Goodloe, John Hogun, James Mhoon, John F. Pride, Nathaniel Pride, H. J. Pride, Dr. Jacob Johnson, M. B. Hampton, Sr., John Lewis Malone, Goodloe W. Malone, Col. Wm. B. Alsobrook, Elijah Hobgood, John Hobgood, Dr. Alexander Sledge, Macklin Sledge and many others of more or less riches.

As I have already said the territory now included in Colbert was a land of great contrasts. There were many large planters in the valley who lived in mansions, dressed fashionably and sent their children to college while back in the hills were many families who lived in small log cabins, wore coarse clothing and whose children got but little if any education. But these latter families were frequently of just as good blood, just as law abiding and just as patriotic as the Valley aristocracy. F. D. Srygley in Chapter X of *"Larimore and His Boys"* discusses very interestingly the contrasts of the average family of the Rock Creek neighborhood where he was born and reared and the rich planters in the valley only a few miles away. According to the 1850 Census report there were over 200 families in what is now Colbert whose real estate value in that year was $1000 and above. Some families whose real estate value was not given or at least the Records were lost in copying and failed to come to my notice. For example Birt Harrington was a large planter of near Tuscumbia in 1850 but I do not have his real estate value. Too much faith should not be put in the census report, for census reports are not always accurate by any means. It is very likely that some persons gave their property above its actual worth and some below. Following is the list of those whose real estate value was shown to be $5,000 and over in 1850:

John G. Shine	$70,000	Wm. W. Downs	15,000
A. Garner	67,220	Robert Goodloe	15,000
F. W. Bynum	60,000	Elijah Hobgood	15,000
Geo. Carroll	60,000	Wm. Jackson	15,000
Drury Vinson	60,000	Richard Prewit	15,000
Abraham Ricks	55,000	John Rand	15,000
Isaac Lane	50,000	Dr. Samuel W. Coons	14,000
Bernard McKiernan	50,000	Joshua Sledge	14,000
Isaac Winston	50,000	Elizabeth Cockburn	12,000
Robert King	40,000	Amos Jarman	12,000
Ann Sherrod	40,000	E. D. Townes	12,000
William Winston	35,000	Robert Warren	12,000
John T. Abernathy	30,000	Thadius Felton	11,000
J. C. Goodloe	30,000	John Alexander	10,000
John Hogun	30,000	Hiberna Armstrong	10,000
James Mhoon	30,000	Azekiah Cobb	10,000
Polly S. Townes	30,000	Lewis Garrett	10,000
Wm. Dickson	29,000	Davis Gurley	10,000
Edward Pearsall	29,000	Martha Harris	10,000
Warren Peden	28,000	John Hobgood	10,000
John F. Pride	26,000	Burchet Curtis King	10,000
Lawrence Thompson	26,000	Elisha Madding	10,000
G. W. Creamer	25,000	Nathaniel Pride	10,000
Dr. Nathaniel Huston	25,000	Whitman Rutland	10,000
Dr. Jacob Johnson	25,000	Macklin Sledge	10,000
Oswald King	25,000	Dr. E. B. Delony	9,000
Goodloe W. Malone	25,000	Albert Guy	9,000
James H. Hogun	21,750	Edward Delony	8,000
Robert Elliott	20,000	Tignal Jones	8,000
Manoah B. Hampton, Sr.	20,000	John T. Morgan	8,000
John Lewis Malone	20,000	James Roberts	7,500
Samuel K. Oats	20,000	Alexander Malone	7,423
James A. Patterson	18,000	Hartwell King, Jr.	7,250
John Kulland	16,500	Robert W. White	7,200
Wm. B. Alsobrook	16,000	Paul King	7,050
Richard Mann	16,000	James Abernathy	7,000
C. A. Toney	16,000	James W. Alexander	7,000
Wm. (E or G?) Bowlin	15,000	James T. Hailey	7,000

James Jackson (aged 56)	7,000	Joseph Askew	5,000
James Jackson (aged 52)	7,000	Jeremiah Burns	5,000
Thomas B. Jenkins	7,000	P. H. Claiburn	5,000
James Long	7,000	Clayton Davidson	5,000
H. J. Pride	7,000	Edmund Ellett	5,000
H. W. Prout	7,000	James W. Higgins	5,000
James Throckmorton	7,000	John Kumpe	5,000
Stephen Winston	6,500	Drury Mayes	5,000
Thomas Austin	6,000	Asa Messenger	5,000
S. O. Eggleston	6,000	Mariah Murphy	5,000
Manerva Haris	6,000	Nicholas Parrish	5,000
Wm. Pride	6,000	Edward Penick	5,000
Isaac Walker	6,000	Wm. R. Person	5,000
A. J. Turner	5,500	Geo. D. Ragland	5,000
Thomas Gibbs	5,300	Samuel Ragland	5,000

There is some doubt as to the real estate value of Mrs. Amanda Barton. Mrs. Gandrud who furnished me 1850 Census information states that it is not clear in the original writing whether it was $127,000 or $27,000. The latter would appear nearer right, as $127,000 seems too far removed from Mr. John G. Shine, whose real estate value was listed as $70,000. Mr. Shine was the highest if we put Mrs. Barton's real estate as $27,000.

I have pointed out the fact that either North Carolina, Tennessee, Virginia, South Carolina, Kentucky or Georgia was the birthplace of the majority of the pioneers of Colbert County. But it might be surprising to know how many prominent men and women of the county before 1875 were born north of the Mason-Dixon line, or were born in foreign countries. Following is a partial list of the former:

Solomon Allen—Massachusetts
Geo. W. Creamer—Pennsylvania
David Deshler—Pennsylvania
George Geise—Pennsylvania
Philip G. Godley—New Jersey
Mrs. P. G. Godley—New Jersey
Samuel Hindman—Pennsylvania
John Kahl—Pennsylvania
Malinda Kahl—Pennsylvania
Col. James McDonald—Ohio
Asa Messenger—Connecticut
John Morton—Maine
Charles Palmer—New York
Philip Palmer—New York
James A. Patterson—Ohio
John Pollock—Massachusetts
Friend Rutherford—New York
George Rutherford—New York
George Ritter—Pennsylvania
James A. Stoddard—Connecticut
Lucinda Stoddard—New York
James Throckmorton—New Jersey
Margaret Throckmorton—New Jersey
Thomas Trowbridge—New York
Prof. Wm. G. Williams—Massachusetts
Samuel Wilson—Pennsylvania

Of those born in foreign lands I shall list the following:

John Andrews—Ireland
Eliza Andrews—Ireland
John Baxter—Ireland
Ann Carroll Baxter—Ireland
Mary Bennett—Ireland
John Bradshaw—England
M. B. Brady—Ireland
Abraham Bresler—Breslau, Russia?
Thomas Brown—England
James Carmack—Ireland
James Crawford—Ireland
Samuel Davis—England
Dr. Wm. Desprez—France
Mrs. Wm. Desprez—Ireland
Mrs. David Deshler—England
Isabella Elliott—Ireland
B. Gledall—England
Edward Gorman—Ireland
James Gorman—Ireland
Lewis Hart—Germany
Joseph Hart—Germany
George S. Henderson—Scotland
Anna J. Henderson—Scotland
Joseph Hillman—Germany
F. D. Hodgkins—England
Samuel Keaghy—Ireland
Dr. Geo. E. Kumpe—Germany
John Kumpe—Germany
Jane Leckey (Mrs. Z. T. Higdon)—Ireland
Alexander Leckey—Ireland
Hugh C. Leckey—Ireland
David Ross Lindsay—Scotland
Robert Burns Lindsay—Scotland
William McCormack—Ireland
Mrs. Wm. McCormack—Ireland
Bernard McKiernan—Ireland
Frank Moron—Ireland
James Murdoch—Scotland
Wm. M. Neal—Scotland
Peter Ohlman—Bavaria
Dennis O'Conner—Ireland
David Powers—Ireland
B. Rosenthal—Germany
H. Rosenthal—Germany
T. T. Rowland—England
J. W. Scott—New Brunswick
Chas. Stein—Germany
Hugh Stephens—Ireland
Ann Stephens—Ireland
Ann (Mrs. John) Taylor—England
Robert Warren—Ireland
William Warren—Ireland
Dr. Charles Williams—Ireland

And I shall conclude Section I with a list of Family names found in what is now Colbert County before the year 1875. I realize that the list is far from being complete. It is most likely that a complete list for Colbert County or any other county, covering that particular period can never be obtained. The list follows:

Abernathy, Adams, Aldridge, Alexander, Allen, Alsobrook, Anderson, Andrews, Armistead, Armstrong, Askew, Atkisson, Austin, Auten, Avery, Aycock, Ayres.

Baisden, Baker, Baldwin, Barclay, Barrett, Barton, Baxter, Beaumont, Bell, Bennett, Bickley, Biggs, Black, Blackburn, Blanton, Blocker, Bowen, Braden, Bradley, Bradshaw, Brady, Bresler, Brown, Bryon, Buck, Burcham, Burns, Bynum, Byrd.

Cannon, Cantrell, Carlock, Carlos, Carmack, Carroll, Carter, Cary, Cheatham, Chidester, Chisholm, Christian, Claiburn, Clay, Clounch, Cobb, Coburn,

Cockburn, Cockrill, Cook, Coons, Cooper, Copeland, Cormack, Craig, Creamer, Crittenden, Croom, Cross, Crowell, Croxton, Curry.

Davidson, Davis, Day, Dean, DeFour, DeGraffenreid, Delony, Dent, Deshler, DesPrez, Dial, Dickson, Didlake, Dill, Dillard, Dobbs, Donley, Dotson, Douthit (or maybe Douthat), Downs, Doxey, Duboise, Duncan.

Eggleston, Elkins, Ellett, Elliott, Enlow, Evans, Farley, Felton, Fielder, Finley, Fort, Foster, Fowler.

Gadd, Galbraith, Gargis, Garner, Garrett, Gassaway, Geise, Gibbs, Gilbert, Gill, Gillean, Gipson, Gledall, Goins, Goodloe, Goodwin, Gorman, Green, Gregg, Greenhill, Grisson, Gurley, Guy.

Halsey, Hampton, Hanks, Hardy, Harrington, Harris, Hart, Henderson, Henry, Hicks, Hillman, Hindman, Hobgood, Hodgkins, Hogun or Hogan, Holesapple, Holley, Hooks, Horn, Hornsby or Hornsbey, Hudson, Hunt, Hunter, Huston, Hyde.

Inman, Isbell.

Jackson, James, Jarman, Jeffreys, Jenkins, Jinx, Johnson, Jones, Julian.

Kahl, Karg, Keaghy, Keenum, Keeton, Keller, Kennerly, Kent, Kilburn, Kimbrough, King, Kumpe.

Lancaster, Landers, Lane, Leckey, Leggett, Leigh, Letsinger, Ligon, Limerick, Lindsay, Lindsey, Long, Looney, Lueddeman.

McAfee, McCaig, McClain, McCleskey, McClung, McCorkle, McCormack, McDaniel, MacDonald, McKee, McKiernan, McKinney, McReynolds, Madding, Malone, Mann, Matlock, Matthews, Mayers, (Meyers according to some), Meredith, Merrill, Messenger, Mhoon, Miller, Mills, Milner, Mitchell, Moody, Moore, Moran, Morton, Moule, Mullens, Murdoch or Murdock, Myatt, Myhan.

Nail, Napier, Neals, Neely, Nelson, Newsom, Newsum, Nichols, Nooe, Norman.

Oats or Oates, O'Conner, Old, Olhman, Oliver, Osborn, Ottaway, Overcash.

Paine, Palmer, Patterson, Patton, Payne, Pearsall, Peden, Penick, Person, Peters, Phillips, Pillar, Pollock, Pope, Porter, Porterfield, Potts, Pounders, Powell, Powers, Prewit or Preuit, Price, Pride, Prince, Prout, Pybas.

Quillen, Quillin.

Ragland, Rand, Rather, Rauhoff, Redwine, Reynolds, Rhea, Richards, Richardson, Ricks, Rikard, Ritter, Roberts, Robinson, Rogers, Rollston, Rosenthal, Ross, Roundall, Rowland, Russell, Rutherford.

Sadler, Saltzer, Sample, Sampson, Sanderson, Sawtelle, Scott, Sevier, Sheffield, Shegog, Sherrod, Shine, Simpson, Skidmore, Sloan, Southall, Spangler, Spencer, Srygley, Stafford, Stanley, Stebbens, Steele, Steger, Stein, Stephens, Stephenson, Stoddard, Sturch, Sugg, Sutherland

Tapp, Tartt, Taylor, Teas, Tharp, Thatcher, Thomas, Thompson, Thorn, Thornton, Throckmorton, Tickle, Tompkins, Toney, Townes, Trabue, Trotter, Trowbridge, Truelove, Tubbaville, Tubb or Tubbs, Turner, Tutwiler.

Underwood, Vandiver, Vinson.

Waddell, Wadsworth, Wagnon, Walker, Wall, Wanner, Warren, Wheeler, White, Whitley, Whitlock, Wilburn, Wilson, Williams, Wingo, Winstead, Winston, Winter, Witt, Womble, Wright.

Yarbrough, Yocom, Young.

COLBERTIANS

SECTION II. SPECIAL SCORE OF FAMILIES

In this section 20 Colbert County families, all who lived in the county at some time before 1875, are discussed rather fully. I want it strictly understood that I do not mean that these twenty families are better than any other twenty that could have been selected. But I believe on the whole they are as good and as interesting as any twenty that could have been selected. This list includes some of the best known professional families, some of the wealthiest families, some of the oldest families and I believe some of as religious and moral families as lived in Colbert County before the War. Some of the characters however, were far from perfection. But I realize that we all have our faults and I have not thought it proper to designate any one as being rather immoral.

SPECIAL SCORE LIST OF FAMILIES

I. THE ELISHA MADDING FAMILY

Elisha Madding died December 4, 1852 aged 70 years. His wife was Eliza Maria Wren Croom. She was born April 10, 1808 and died January 1, 1888. Their children were: 1. Mary Ann married Charles Augustus Toney. 2. Richard Thomas. 3. James Allen, married Elizabeth Langston Christian. 4. Eliza Jane married Philemon King. 5. Robert Franklin. 6. Isaac Croom. 7. Camilla Wilmarth married (1) Dr. James T. Jones (2) Capt. A. D. Coffee, a son of General John Coffee of Creek War fame. 8. Edwin Price died in his twelfth year.

II. THE EDWARD PEARSALL FAMILY

According to the 1850 census report Edward Pearsall was born about 1784 and according to a statement in his wife's obituary he died about 1853. His wife was Parthenia Shearan or Shearon. She was born March 12, 1800 and died December 23, 1871. Their children included: 1. Elizabeth married Samuel Elliott. 2. Anne married a Mr. Eve or Eves? 3. Thomas Ella married Hon. J. Burns Moore. 4. Catherine married Dr. John Rand. 5. Sarah Letitia married Hon. John D. Rather (his second wife). 6. Nathan was married twice. Name of first wife unknown (2) Mrs. Sherrod. 7. Edward, Jr. There may have been one or two others who died in infancy.

III. THE HARTWELL KING SR. FAMILY

Hartwell King Sr. (Hartwell Richard King to use his full name) was born March 1, 1785 and died September 3, 1841. His wife was Burchet Curtis. She was born February 10, 1785 and died October 22, 1872. Their children were: 1. Oswald married Martha Rebecca Delony. 2. Robert married Margaret Pick. 3. Mary Curtis married James Fennel. 4. Susan married Tignal Jones. 5. Philemon married Eliza Jane Madding. 6. Martha Burchet married (1) Thadius Felton (2) Tignal Jones. Mr. Felton had died and so had Mrs. Susan Jones, so later Mrs. Felton married her brother in law, Tignal Jones. 7. Hartwell Richard, Jr. married Mary Henderson Smith. 8. Paul H. married Mary Cummins. 9. Washington Lafayette died in childhood. 10. Ann Lafayette Sr. died in infancy. 11. Ann LaFayette married Prof. Edward Goodwin.

IV. THE DRURY VINSON FAMILY

Drury Vinson was born March 4, 1788 and died May 31, 1862.

His wife was Mary Curtis. She was born April 14, 1792 and died September 12, 1877. Their children were: 1. Martha Ann died when fifteen or sixteen. 2. John died young. 3. Fletcher Curtis married (1) Mosley Ann Rand, his first cousin. (2). Annie H. Berry.

V. THE BIRT HARRINGTON FAMILY

Birt Harrington appears to have been born about the year 1790. I know that he died May 18, 1860. His wife was Harriet C. Johnston. She was born June 1, 1798 and died October 14, 1873. Their children included 1. Frances married Hon. Lydal Bacon Cooper. 2. Samuel J. said to have been twice married and perhaps a child who died in infancy. One of Samuel J. Harrington's wives was Harriet Adelia Jarmon but I do not know who the other one was.

VI. THE ABRAHAM RICKS FAMILY

Abraham Ricks was born October 16, 1791 and died November 23, 1852. His wife was his first cousin, Charlotte Bryant Fort. She was born December 29, 1795 and died March 19, 1874. Their children were: 1. William F. married (1) Ann Elizabeth Allison, a native of Limestone County, Alabama (2) a Miss Fields from Mississippi. 2. Richard Henry. 3. Abram married Sallie Pope of Spring Valley.

VII. THE JAMES W. LIGON FAMILY

James W. Ligon was born May 28, 1797 and died July 27, 1882. His wife was Mary Gannaway. She was born March 31, 1801 and died March 4, 1877. Among their children were: 1. Abner W. married (1) Rebecca E. Smith (2) Mrs. Ida Crawford nee Patterson. 2. Nancy married (1) Thomas Skidmore (2) Dr. J. S. Napier. 3. Adline married Asa Cobb. 4. Williams. 5. Amelia married (1) .... Burton (2) Thomas East. There may have been other children. William Ligon married and had children but as yet I do not know who his wife was.

VIII. THE HECTOR ATKISSON FAMILY

Hector Atkisson, according to his tombstone record, was born

March 7, 1798 (his obituary says 1797) and died October 11, 1871. His wife was Sallie Franklin. She was born May 20, 1805 and died September 25, 1859. Their children included 1. Caroline H. 2. Joel Ann married John E. Donley. 3. Sallie W. B. 4. Arthur married (1) Susan Donley (2) Lucy Sherrod. 5. Martha Jane married John E. Donley. 6. Mary M. married Tilmon A. Whitley. 7. Hester M. married John E. Donley. 8. Hectoria C. married Robert Milton Garner. 9. Rebecca L. married Robert P. Moore.

IX. THE WILLIAM COOPER FAMILY

William Cooper was born January 11, 1802 and died August 16, 1887. He was married three times. His first wife was Susan McCulloch. His second wife was Elizabeth Blocker. His third wife was Mrs. Julia Blocker nee Plummer. His first wife died September 6, 1834 aged 30 years. His second wife died April 8, 1868 aged 50 years. I do not know the birth or death date of the third Mrs. Cooper. The children of William and Susan McCulloch Cooper were: 1. Langston died in 1850 unmarried. 2. Jane married James T. Pettit. 3. James Parks married (1) Elizabeth Stoddard (2) wife unknown.

The children of William and Elizabeth Blocker Cooper were: 1. John William married Anna Shine. 2. Susan McCulloch married Wm. A. Nelson. 3. Sarah Amelia married John Goodwin. 4. Mollie Rufus married Benjamin R. Winter. 5. Julia Frances married Eldon R. Rather. 6. Anna Langston died in infancy.

X. THE JAMES A. STODDARD FAMILY

James A. Stoddard was born May 24, 1804 and died February 20, 1874. He was twice married. His first wife was Lucinda Lawrence. She was born May 11, 1819 and died May 12, 1841? His second wife was Isabella G. Green. She died May 15, 1883 aged 55? Mr. Stoddard's children by his first wife included 1. Lizzie married Dr. J. P. Cooper. 2. Lucy married Dr. Chas. Bell and 3. child who died in infancy. Mr. Stoddard's children by his second wife included 1. Hattie C. married W. M. Wiley. 2. Ellen D. married Chas. F. Bowen and 3. a son who died in infancy.

I am not positively sure that Mr. Stoddard's first wife was a Lawrence as the inscription on her slab is dim. But I believe

Lawrence is correct. I do not know where the infant children came in acording to age, so I put them last.

XI. THE JAMES THROCKMORTON FAMILY

James Throckmorton was born in 1809 and died 1874. He was married twice. His first wife was Margaret Polhemus and his second wife was Mary Miller Ellett. Margaret Polhemus was born August 4, 1813 and died July 8, 1850. Mary Miller Ellett was born June 11, 1830 and died December 13, 1917. The children of the first marriage were 1. Craig married Annie Newnum. 2. Julia married Robert A. Goodloe, Jr. 3. Helen married (1) John Person (2) Duane Guernsey. The children of the second marriage were: 1. Edmund Ellett married (1) Mary McCleksey (2) Jennie Armistead. 2. Thomas C. married Mrs. Pattie Wilbourn nee Armistead. 3. Jennie married Hugh Henderson. 4. Mamie married Mr. Wall. I am not sure as to Mr. Wall's first name. Miss Julia Throckmorton who furnished me much of the Throckmorton data thought that his first name was Lacy or Lacey, but in the obituary of Mrs. Mary Miller Throckmorton, he is referred to as A. C. Wall.

XII. THE EDWARD H. NEWSOM FAMILY

I was unable to obtain the birth and death dates of Mr. and Mrs. Edward H. Newson. Mrs. Newson was Penelope Rutland. Their children included five sons and four daughters. The sons were: 1. Whit, never married. 2. Charles E. married Mollie Ligon. 3. John E. married Mattie Brandon. 4. William B. married Mary Anna Woodford. 5. Millard married, but name of wife unknown.

The daughters were: 1. Mollie married R. D. Nelson. 2. Lallie Virginia married J. C. Holesapple. 3. Fannie m. (1) William? Woodford (2) R. D. Nelson (the first Mrs. Nelson who was her sister had died). 4. Elizabeth married I. P. Guy.

XIII. THE NATHANIEL WHITLOCK FAMILY

Nathaniel Whitlock was born June 24, 1813 and died January 15, 1885. His wife was Ellenar C. Tackett. She "died July 21, 1914 age 83 years". They had one child, Charley M. Whitlock. He married Nancy Gargis.

XIV. THE L. B. COOPER FAMILY

Lydal Bacon Cooper was born December 12, 1813 and died March 21, 1892. His wife was Frances Harrington a daughter of Birt and Harriet C. (Johnston) Harrington. Their children were: 1. Birt Harrington married Elizabeth Hogun. 2. Martha married Richard L. Ross. 3. J. Parks married Mattie Halsey. 4. Dr. Samuel J. married Jennie Pettit. 5. Dr. William married Mattie Wells. 6. Harriet married Prof. A. A. McGregor. 7. Langston M. died unmarried.

XV. THE CHARLES WOMBLE FAMILY

Charles Womble was born October 22, 1818 and died June 16, 1876. His wife was Mary M. Curry. She was born November 30, 1818 and died April 25, 1903. Their children were: 1. Sarah Jane married Obadiah Chisholm. 2. Martha Mildred died young. 3. William Amos married Susan Reed. 4. John Leman died in infancy. 5. Isaac Newton married Ellen V. Page. 6. Elizabeth Frances married Dan Moody. 7. Mary Louisa married Dr. Parkerson Carter. 8. Charles Adolphus married Lucy B. McReynolds. 9 Johannah married Burnett Carter, a cousin of Dr. Parkerson Carter. 10. Dayton Graves never married. He was killed in a shooting affray with Policeman Gipson in Tuscumbia on August 26, 1889. 11. James Alexander married (1) a Miss Noland (2) unknown.

XVI. THE O. H. PERRY WILLIAMS FAMILY

Oliver Hazard Perry Williams was born March 1, 1822 and died November 15, 1903. His wife was Mary Garrett. She was born February 24, 1824 and died May 18, 1880. Their children were: 1. Henry married Emma Carr. 2. Dr. Charley F. married Mollie Alexander. 3. James William married Cornelia Carmichael. 4. T. Wesley married (1) Bettie Avery (2) Anna Gregory. 5. Alice married Chas. F. Turner. 6. Ida married Willie Harris.

XVII. THE WM. REESE JULIAN FAMILY

William Reese Julian was born in December, 1822, and died August 23, 1889. His wife was Elizabeth Melissia Croxton. She was born April 25, 1836 and died May 13, 1904. Their children were: 1. Henrie Scott died young. 2. Owen Nelson married Mary McReynolds. 3. William Croxton. 4. Ellen Lavinia married George Black. 5. Milton Croxton. 6. Charley Minta. 7. Frank Newsum married a Miss Stephenson.

XVIII. THE JAMES H. SRYGLEY FAMILY

James H. Srygley was born August 16, 1824 and died October 30, 1906. His wife was Sarah Jane Coats. She was born November 7, 1831 and died August 20, 1899. She and Mr. Srygley were married on October 28, 1844. They had five sons and four daughters. The sons were: 1. Felix Grundy married (1) Susan Oden (2) Mrs. Beckey Butts. 2. Fernando Wallace married Ann Sandlin. 3. Fletcher Douglass married (1) Ella Parkhill (2) Jennie Scobey. 4. Filo Bunyan married Mary Hubbard. 5. Floyd Lamar married Sally Miller.

The daughters were: 1. Dona Ann Martha Minerva Constance Louisa Jane married John Wallis. She was named in honor of seven aunts which acounts for her name of seven parts. 2. Chestena Arkansas married Andrew Hill. 3. Lauda married T. Miller Blankenship. 4. Dora J. married R. A. Hill.

XIX. THE J. BURNS MOORE FAMILY

Joshua Burns Moore was born March 11, 1826 and died March 15, 1897. His wife was Thomas Ella Pearsall. She was born December 24, 1840 and died November 22, 1874. Their children consisted of four daughters as follows: 1. Susie Erle married Dr. John M. Shaller. 2. Annie Lee. 3. Nina. 4. Ella Burns.

XX. THE THEOPHILUS COBURN FAMILY

I do not know the birth date of Theophilus Coburn. His grandson Paul Coburn, Colbert's present Representative in the Legislature, advises me that he died in 1884. His wife, whose maiden name was Neomie Howard, survived him several years, but I do not have the dates of her birth and death. The children of Mr. and Mrs. Coburn who lived to adult life were: 1. William T. married (1) Martha A. Barham (2) ? Grissom. 2. Ernest married (1) Estelle McCulloch (2) Mattie Hooper (3) Lula Townsend. 3. Percy S. married Katie Kirkland. 4. James married

Mary McCulloch. 5. Frances married (1) John Hooper (2) James Tubbs. 6. Theophilus Bester married Katie Richardson. 7. Maury married Effie Fort.

REVIEWING THE SPECIAL SCORE FAMILIES

Now let us take a general review or study of the Special Score Families and their relation to others. There were of the men and their wives 44 characters. There were of course twenty men and of these twenty, Hon. William Cooper was married three times, Mr. James A. Stoddard was married twice and Mr. James Throckmorton was married twice. A thing that rather interests me is the great difference in some of the ages of the men and their wives. Elisha Madding was more than 25 years older than his wife, James A. Stoddard was 15 years, or practically so, older than his first wife and with a still greater contrast between his age and that of his second wife, James Throckmorton was more than 20 years older than his second wife, Wm. Reese Julian was more than 13 years older than his wife, and J. Burns Moore was in his seventeenth year when Thomas Ella Pearsall was born. Sarah Jane Coats was a thirteen year old girl when she became the wife of James H. Srygley, who was seven years older than she. One of her granddaughters advises me that she was so much of a child that she often forgot to get dinner until Mr. Srygley came in from the field. Yet she made a faithful wife and became the mother of a brilliant family of children.

Four of the twenty men composing the Special Score Families —Edmond Pearsall, Hartwell King Sr., Drury Vinson, and Abraham Ricks, were born in North Carolina, four—Elisha Madding, James W. Ligon, Hector Atkisson, and Wm. Cooper were born in Virginia and four—Lydal B. Cooper, Charles Womble, O. H. Perry Williams, and Theophilus Coburn are said to have been born in Tennessee. At least three—Wm. Reese Julian, James H. Srygley and J. Burns Moore were Alabamians by birth the first two being natives of Lawrence County and the last of Franklin County having been reared near Duncan Creek Church a few miles west of Russellville. Nathaniel Whitlock is said to have come from Fayette County, Alabama, but he was probably born in South Carolina. Mr. Whitlock was also more than 17 years older than Ellenar Tacket. If he had been married previously, I have no record of it. Of the four remaining men, James A. Stoddard was born in Connecticut (Litchfield County), James Throckmorton in New Jersey, and Birt Harrington and Edward H. Newsom came from South Carolina and I suppose were born there.

In regard to where the twenty four wives of the Special Score Families were born I am advised that Mrs. Elisha Madding, Mrs. Edward Pearsall, Mrs. Hartwell King, Sr., Mrs. Drury Vinson and Mrs. Abraham Ricks were North Carolinians. It appears that Mrs. Birt Harrington, Mrs. Edward H. Newsom, Mrs. Lydal B. Cooper and Mrs. Wm. Reese Julian were all South Carolinians. The first wife of James A. Stoddard was born in Brooklyn, New York, and his second wife, was, I believe, born in Tuscumbia. The first wife of James Throckmorton was a native of Mount Holly, New Jersey, and I believe his second wife was perhaps born near Spring Valley in Colbert County. Mrs. Hector Atkisson, was, I suppose, a native of Virginia. I know that she and Mr. Atkisson lived there after they were married and before coming to Alabama. I am advised that Mrs. Theophilus Coburn was born in Tennessee and Mrs. James W. Ligon and Mrs. O. H. Perry Williams were probably born in Tennessee.

The homes of the Special Score Families were as follows: Elisha Madding and Hartwell King, Sr. lived in the *Town Creek-Triangle*, the former living north of the Tuscumbia and Decatur Railroad (now part of the Southern) and the latter south of it. The Madding home was east or a little northeast of Leighton and the King home was southeast. Mr. King also had a residence at LaGrange and Mr. Madding may have had one there. Edward Pearsall, Wm. Cooper, Lydal Cooper, J. B. Moore and Wm. Reese Julian lived in Tuscumbia or very near there. The Pearsall home I believe was outside of the city limits. The Coopers, Mr. Moore and Mr. Julian lived "right in town." James W. Ligon's last days were spent in Tuscumbia and he and Mrs. Ligon are buried in Tuscumbia's Oakwood Cemetery. But he lived for years in the southern edge of the county at Ligon's Springs and other places in the neighborhood of Ligon's Springs. James A. Stoddard lived in Tuscumbia but I think he lived for sometime near Bear Creek Church a few miles southwest of Tuscumbia. I know his widow lived there. Drury Vinson's home was about two miles west, or a little southwest of Leighton, and some two miles southwest of his home was the home of Abraham Ricks. The Ricks family's post office was LaGrange, on the mountain, and perhaps not over a mile and a half, or two miles "as the crow flies", Hector Atkisson lived some two miles south of Barton near where Mountain Mills Factory was later erected. James Throckmorton's home was on the Tuscumbia and Frankfort Road about two miles, or perhaps a little more, out of Tuscumbia. He may have at some time lived in Tuscumbia. Edward H. Newsom lived about two miles east of Cherokee and O. H. Perry Williams lived to the south of Cherokee. Nathaniel Whitlock lived a little east of Fox-trap Creek near the present Colbert-Franklin line.

And I am here going to "switch from the main line" for a wee bit. The place where Mr. Whitlock lived is a pretty place, commanding a fine view to the south and west. Mr. Whitlock, as I understand it, settled the place, and there reared his only child, Charley M. Whitlock who was a commissioner from Colbert's Southeast District, when a very young man and was later tax collector of the county. Charley M. Whitlock married a daughter of Henry Gargis who lived on Poplar Creek and lived with his parents in his early married life. After Nathaniel Whitlock died, Charley M. Whitlock and his family including his mother, moved to the Brick community north of Leighton. The Nathaniel Whitlock farm passed into the hands of W. J. Phagan from Georgia. In 1903 Mr. Phagan and Mr. J. E. Felton of Leighton traded property; and the latter and his family lived at this place two or three years. Mr. Felton's aged and venerable mother, then the widow of Tignal Jones, removed from Leighton with her son and his family and died there Sept. 17, 1904, the last of the distinguished family of Hartwell King Sr. There have been a number of other families who lived at the Nathaniel Whitlock place including the Lafayette Mayfield family who lived there many years. Nathaniel Whitlock was buried in the cemetery at Bethlehem in Franklin County but not very far from his home. His mother-in-law, Celia Tackett, was buried at Bethlehem in 1873 having been born in 1807. In the 1850 Census report of Franklin, which included what is now Colbert, exclusive of the Town Creek-Triangle, a number of Tackett families were listed. There was Sugar Tackett and Coffee Tackett. If there had been a Cream Tackett the naming would have been prefect. And in conclusion of this detour I wish to say that there was a Baptist preacher named John Whitlock, who lived on Fox-trap Creek in Colbert, but I do not know what his relation was to Nathaniel Whitlock.

Birt Harrington's home was some distance east of Tuscumbia; James H. Srygley lived near the present Rock Creek Church and School at the place where Mr. John Hill now lives; Charles Womble lived at Tuscumbia or at least near there, and Theophilus Coburn's home was near Hunter post office and Mount Moriah Church. A son of Mr. Coburn now lives at the old homestead. It is my understanding that COBURNS have lived continuously there ever since Theophilus Coburn settled there before the War. Not many such records can be found but there is at least one other in Colbert that heads it. The place where Abraham Ricks lived and died has been the home of RICKES ever since he first settled there. The name at both the Coburn and Ricks places has not changed.

GENERAL DISCUSSION OF THE SPECIAL SCORE

FAMILIES

The Elisha Madding family was a family of splendid character, culture and wealth. Perhaps the War of Secession hit this family as hard a blow as any family in what is now Colbert County. It took three out of four promising young men and probably shortened the life of the fourth one several years.

The head of the family, Elisha Madding, came from Virginia so states his granddaughter, Mrs. James Smith of Leighton, Alabama. His wife was a daughter of Dr. Richard Croom from North Carolina, who removed to what is now Hale County, Alabama. Mr. Madding settled in the *Town Creek-Triangle* at a fairly early date. Col. J. E. Saunders said this about Mr. (or Capt.) Madding as a young man—"He was a young man of very fine person, good manners and great energy. He accumulated a handsome fortune for himself, married a daughter of Dr. Croom, one of three or four brothers who were wealthy and came from North Carolina nearly sixty years ago."

And of him in later life he said: "Captain Madding was a man of fine sense—Elisha Madding died some years ago, much respected by all who knew him for his integrity and many virtues."

The sons of Elisha and Eliza Madding, who lost their lives in the War were Richard Thomas, Isaac Croom and Robert Franklin. The first of the trio had his thigh broken at the Battle of Shiloh. His leg was amputated and he died at Corinth, Mississippi soon after the Battle of Chickamauga and Robert Franklin "was killed in the trenches near Atlanta by a shot from a Federal sharp shooter". Isaac Croom Madding had prepared to be a lawyer and Robert Franklin Madding had graduated in medicine at the University of Louisiana. These brothers had formerly been students in LaGrange College. Some one said of Isaac Croom Madding: "He was well educated, brave and high-minded, and in person eminently handsome."

James Allen Madding, the son who survived the war, was made prisoner during the time and had a severe spell of sickness. After the war was over he went to the battlefields and took up the bodies of his brothers and had them interred in the Madding family cemetery. In this he was assisted by faithful negro servants who had accompanied his brothers on the battlefields, so I am informed by Mrs. Smith. James Allen Madding was the only son of Elisha and Eliza Madding who lived to marry. His wife was Elizabeth Langston Christian, a daughter of John Tate Christian, a Tuscumbia merchant, who came from Virginia. The mother of Eizabeth Langston Christian was a daughter of Charles Cooper of Tuscumbia. (The name "Langston" was widely used through the Cooper family.) Five daughters were born to James Allen Madding and wife, and all of these married; and perhaps all had issue except Annie Christian who married Prof. J. S. Hawkins and died within a few months after marriage. The youngest one of the five Madding sisters has her father's name in full. James Allen Madding was born June 7, 1832 and died Sept. 20, 1880. Mrs. Elizabeth Langston Madding was born August 3, 1847 and died Sept. 8, 1911.

In regard to the wife of Elisha Madding and her three daughters I shall refer again to Col. Saunders. Of Mrs. Eliza Madding he said: "The 'mother of the Gracchi,' who gave all her sons to her country still lives—the same unpretending, kind, true-hearted Christian woman she ever was, performing faithfully her duties in the private circle, as they nobly theirs before the world on the battlefield."

The three daughters all married into noted families. Mary Ann and Eliza Jane each became the mother of many children.

Col. Saunders said of Camilla Wilmarth, the youngest girl, "Camilla grew up with much beauty and a queenly person—a discreet, sweet-tempered, graceful and cultivated woman". She was the one who was twice married. Here is an extract from the obituary of Dr. James T. Jones, her first husband, who died April 7, 1872 in his forty-eighth year. "His success was built upon the strictest integrity, honor, honesty and uprightness, always scorning that which was mean or selfish. He had endeared himself to all who knew him."

The obituary of Dr. Jones is in *"Alabamian & Times"*, published at Tuscumbia, for April 11, 1872.

Edward Pearsall who lived at, or near, Tuscumbia for many years before the War had mighty good blood in his veins, and was related to a host of noted people. His wife was also said to have been a woman of superb Christian character. To illustrate the kind of father Edward Pearsall had, I shall quote an incident related by Col. J. E. Saunders in his *"Early Settlers"*. On pages 199 and 200 of that book the Colonel said:

"Jeremiah Pearsall moved his family to this county (Lawrence County) about 1821. . . . The Pearsalls were good Presbyterian people, cultivated, refined and hospitable. The head of this family not only squared his conduct by the law, but by the golden rule. I remember that a horse trader, one spring, offered him a plow horse for one hundred dollars, extolling his good qualities. Mr. Pearsall had doubts as to his value, and offered ninety dollars for him, payable in the fall, and bought him. When the driver came for his money the old gentleman paid him the full price of one hundred dollars, saying that the horse was found, on trial, to be every thing the trader said he was."

Jeremiah Pearsall had several children besides Edward. Among them was James M. Pearsall for many years a commission merchant in New Orleans, and a daughter, Dolly, who married Metcalfe De Graffenreid, and at least two other daughters, Catherine who married a Mr. Bronson from Tennessee and a daughter whose name I do not know, but who was remarkably "beautiful in person, and lovely in character." She first married a man by name of Camp. Mr. Camp did not live very long, and as a young widow,

Mrs. Camp was sought by many suitors. Finally she married Nathan Gregg and became the mother of a most prominent family of children. The Gregg family lived for a while at LaGrange where Mr. and Mrs. Gregg had charge of the mess hall at LaGrange College. I shall now quote from McGregor's history of LaGrange College:

"Mr. Nathan Gregg, Sr., a staunch Presbyterian, succeeded Mrs. Harris and was steward until 1849. Mr. Gregg had four sons, John, James, Edward and Nathan, and one daughter. John and James graduated in 1847. Edward did not graduate. Nathan graduated in 1850. Mr. John Gregg went to Fairfield, Texas and became a district judge of much eminence. He was a brigadier general in the Confederate army, and was killed October 7, 1863 in the battle before Richmond, at the New Market road.

"His wife went to Virginia after his body and had it buried at Aberdeen, Miss. She was Miss Mollie Garth, a daughter of Gen. Garth who lived near Decatur, Ala. Nathan Gregg, Jr. died in a few months after graduation."

General John Gregg was truly a remarkable character. Col. Saunders advises us that upon his graduation from LaGrange College, Prof. Tutwiler selected him to teach languages and mathematics at Green Springs Academy, a position which he accepted and held for four years.

Now back to Edward Pearsall and his immediate family. He was quite a wealthy man and was no doubt a leading citizen. He was commissioned a Justice of Peace on March 3, 1823, when many others were commissioned at the same time. Mr. Pearsall was married before coming to Alabama. He and his wife were married in east Tennessee. Mrs. Pearsall was a native of Warren County, North Carolina. She was a member of the Presbyterian church for many years and was said to have been of excellent character.

The children of Edward and Parthenia Pearsall married into prominent families, and as far as I know, they themselves were all of splendid character. The sons-in-law were indeed quite a brilliant galaxy—Gen. John D. Rather, Hon. J. Burns Moore, Dr. John Rand, Mr. Samuel Elliott and Mr. Eve. Tuscumbia had few, if any citizens more distinguished than Mr. Rather and Mr.

Moore. Mr. Elliott was a wealthy planter of near Trinity and had a rather princely estate called "Boxwood". I am advised that the Memphis and Charleston Railroad Company awarded him a lovely trophy for having the best kept estate on that division of the road. The Rands were among the best known people of North Alabama. I do not have any particular data on Mr. Eve (or Eves) but I suppose he had an interesting background.

I have no information available regarding Edward and Parthenia Pearsall's son, Nathan. Their son, Edward, died at sea. Miss Mary Wallace Kirk, a granddaughter of Gen. Rather and Letitia Pearsall, says he had been to California and was returning by way of Cape Horn, when fatal illness overtook him. He was going to be a lawyer.

The family of Hartwell King Sr. has indeed been one of note in the Leighton and LaGrange communities. Perhaps no family in Colbert County had a better combination of integrity, culture and wealth than the King family. Prof. McGregor in his *"History of LaGrange College"* had the following to say of Hartwell King, Sr.:

"Mr. Hartwell King Sr. was a large planter whose home was in the valley about six miles east of LaGrange. He had a large family and was a public spirited man and much interested in the cause of education. He was one of the charter members of the board of trustees of LaGrange College, and was a member of that body until his death. He was born March 1, 1785 in Wake County, N. C. and moved to Lawrence County, Ala. in 1826. He died September 3, 1841. He was a very industrious man, noted for his financial ability and good judgment in all business transactions. He brought some property with him from North Carolina, but during the years he lived in Alabama he raised a large family and amassed a large estate. Besides caring for his own business he was more than once a member of the state legislature and was always a strong advocate for all—bills looking to the interest of the people."

Mr. King's father was Richard King (1752-1830) and his mother was a Miss Jones. He had, I believe one sister who was a great deal younger than himself, and who married a man named Geo. H. Hinton. Mrs. Hartwell King is said to have been a fine character. I have seen her picture and also the picture of Hartwell

King, Sr. Mrs. King's picture was taken in her advanced age but it shows her to have been of a strong mold of character. If Hartwell King Sr.'s picture represents him correctly he was unusually handsome, and a very distinguished looking gentleman. According to his portrait, his son, Philemon, was also very fine looking. He was the only one of the sons of Hartwell and Burchet King whose picture I have seen. Mrs. Philemon King, the former Eliza Jane Madding, was a very beautiful woman.

Mr. and Mrs. Hartwell King Sr., Mr. King's father (and perhaps his mother), all the sons of Mr. and Mrs. Hartwell King, Sr. and their wives, their youngest daughter, Mrs. Ann Goodwin and her husband, Col. Goodwin, besides many grandchildren and other relatives are buried in the King cemetery, which is near the former King residence in the Town Creek-Triangle. This is the largest family cemetery that I know anything about in Colbert County. However, three of Mr. and Mrs. King's daughters are not buried there. The eldest, Mrs. Mary Fennel, is buried in the Fennel cemetery near Trinity, the second, Mrs. Susan Jones, is buried in Texas, and the third, Mrs. Burchet Felton Jones, is buried at LaGrange, as is Mr. Tignal Jones.

The tombstone of Mrs. Oswald King has written on it a rather unique sentiment which I pass on to the reader. Here it is:

> "Could love and friendship have
> retained her, Martha, would still have been
> of earth, but Heaven claimed its own
> and her Spirit winged its flight above."

She was Martha Rebecca Delony, the daughter of Capt. Edward Delony who lived at LaGrange in order to educate his children. She was a student of Dr. D. P. Bester; and she was the mother of Prof. Robert King both a graduate and Professor of LaGrange College. She was born June 26, 1811 and died Oct. 31, 1851.

It appears that all of Hartwell and Burchet King's sons were successful in a financial way and all married into influential families. I do not have information on all of them, however, Col. J. E. Saunders refers to the Cummins family into which Paul H. King married. His wife's father was once clerk of the Circuit Court in

Lawrence County. Col. Saunders said: "A J. M. Cummins lived east of Moulton when I first knew him. He was then a militia Major, and had great fondness for Regimental musters. After that, he became an able Missionary Baptist preacher. . . . . he had a very pretty, intelligent daughter, who married my neighbor, Paul King, they are both dead."

The daughters of Hartwell and Burchet King married men of note. Mary and her husband, James Fennel, were rather closely related. She outlived him more than 37 years. Mrs. Fennel was one of Dr. D. P. Bester's honor graduates and later assisted him in teaching. The Fennel family into which she married also came from North Carolina, but they settled near Trinity. This Fennel family lived in quite different style from the one referred to in Thomas Hardy's *"The Three Strangers"*. Tignal Jones and Thadeus Felton were also from North Carolina and were prominent citizens. The Feltons had a rather large family connection about Leighton and LaGrange. Col. Goodwin who married Ann, the youngest of all the King family, was a son of John Goodwin, a distinguished Aberdeen, Mississippi, lawyer. He graduated at LaGrange College and was one of its most ambitious Professors for several years. He and his wife at that time lived with her mother in the *Town Creek-Triangle,* about six miles from the college. He rode horseback much of the time and was always on time to meet his classes. He also saw after home affairs and wrote during the time a novel entitled *"Lily White."* He helped organize the 35th Alabama Reg. of Infantry at LaGrange in 1862. He became Lieutenant Colonel of the regiment. He died while attending a court martial at Columbus, Mississippi, in 1863. He was buried in Aberdeen but "in December, 1865, his body was disinterred at the request of his widow, brought to his old home and reburied in the King cemetery." His widow survived him more than 38 years. Col. Goodwin was just a little past 33 years of age when he died.

Of the many grandchildren of Hartwell and Burchet King, Dr. John Curtis Jones was perhaps the most distinguished. He was a son of Tignal and Susan Jones, a native (formerly) of Lawrence County, and a graduate of LaGrange College in the 1856 class. He studied medicine abroad and attained to a very high degree of knowledge in surgery. He was an honored citizen of Gonzales, Texas, where he died January 28, 1904.

As has already been noticed, the family of Drury Vinson was a small one. Mrs. Vinson was a sister of Mrs. Hartwell King, Sr. Mrs. Aldridge Myatt, and Mrs. John Rand Sr. being the youngest of the four sisters. All four of these sisters with their families settled within a few miles of Leighton in the year 1826. Prof. John C. Stephenson said they were all good, industrious women. The writer of Mrs. Vinson's obituary commented on her hospitality. She was a member of the Methodist church from early life. In fact, I believe that all, or nearly all of the Vinsons, Kings, Maddings, Feltons, Fennels, Rands, Myatts and other families about Leighton and LaGrange were Methodists, LaGrange College itself was a Methodist institution.

The most authentic record I have of Drury Vinson is from his tombstone which I here reproduce.

"In memory of

Drury Vinson

Born in Johnston Co. N. C.

March 4, 1788

was married to Mary Curtis Daughter of

John and Mary Curtis Dec. 26, 1811 professed religion &

joined the M. E. church in 1811 & continued faithful &

exemplary member to the end of his life. He moved to

this State in 1826 & Died May 31, 1862."

Of the three children of Mr. and Mrs. Drury Vinson, Martha Ann, born July 3, 1815, was a girl of a lovely personality and a high degree of intelligence. She was the pride and hope of her mother's heart and graduated with first honor at LaGrange in 1830. Within six weeks after her graduation she passed away. The eldest son, John, soon followed his sister Martha Ann, to the grave. The remaining son, Fletcher Curtis Vinson, graduated at LaGrange College and was later a trustee of LaGrange. I believe he was one of the first commissioners of Colbert. He was known as "Col. Vinson" and was at one time quite wealthy. His home in his last years was near the foot of LaGrange Mountain, on the road from LaGrange to Leighton. He died in March 1879.

He was married twice. His first wife was Mosley Ann Rand (1824-1862) and was his first cousin. Annie H. Berry who died in 1900 aged 70 years was his second wife. He had several children by each wife.

Birt Harrington was a prominent planter who lived east of Tuscumbia. He died while on a visit, in Fayette County, Texas, on the 18th of May in 1860 and was buried in the Lone Star State. Mrs. Harrington is buried in Oakwood Cemetery at Tuscumbia. All business houses in Tuscumbia closed for Mrs. Harrington's funeral.

Birt Harrington and wife's two children who lived to adult life were prominent people. The elder of the two, Frances became the wife of Lydal Bacon Cooper, and the younger, Samuel J. Harrington (1822-1885) was one of Colbert's best known citizens. He lived for some time in Texas but the greater portion of his life was spent in the vicinity of Tuscumbia. He was one of Colbert's representatives in the Legislature, but was perhaps best known as a scientific farmer. He wrote on agricultural subjects for scientific publications. Mr. Harrington was a member of the Presbyterian Church and is said to have been a Christian gentleman. He is said to have been married twice. One of his wives was a Texas lady—Harriet Adelia Jarmon. I have not learned the name of the other. Mr. Harrington is buried near his mother in Oakwood.

Abraham Ricks was a son of Isaac and Olivia (or Olive?) (Fort) Ricks of North Carolina. Isaac Ricks was born in Halifax County, N. C. in 1760 and died in 1820. He was called Isaac Ricks III. Olivia Fort, his wife, was born in 1772 and died in 1824. They were married in 1788 and had the following issue:

1. Martha (Patsie) married .... Pierce

2. Orrin died in War of 1812 at Norfolk, Va.

3. Charlotte married John Harris, Jackson, Tenn.

4. Abraham married Charlotte B. Fort

5. Isaac married Mary Gee

6. Richard accidentally killed when 18

7. Mary M. married Munroe Fort

ABRAHAM RICKS

CHARLOTTE BRYANT (FORT) RICKS

8. John Sherrod married _____ Dawson

9. Elizabeth married _____ Sticknay

10. Benjamin Sherrod married Fannie Winter

11. Pheribee married Geo. W. Mayers

12. Robert married Eliza Toney.

As has already been said, Abraham Ricks and his wife were first cousins. Also Mary Ricks, Abraham's sister, married Munroe S. Fort, brother of Abraham's wife. Munroe S. Fort lived east, or northeast of the Abraham Ricks home and I know he is buried at LaGrange. I do not know where Mrs. Fort is buried. The slab over Munroe S. Fort's grave states that he was born in Northampton County, N. C., April 7, 1800, and died December 8, 1848. In Dr. Owen's *"History of Alabama and Dictionary of Alabama Biography"* the name is spelled "Foort". Mr. Abe Ricks tells me that it used to be spelled that way but I believe all the family now spell it "Fort", said that spelling is found on Monroe S. Fort's gravestone. Also Prof. McGregor used the latter spelling in his history of LaGrange College. Pheribee Ricks who married Geo. W. Mayers, also lived northeast of her brother, Abraham Ricks, and about three miles from Leighton for a number of years. This family removed to Louisiana and she died in Bossier Parish in 1877. The account of her death in the "North Alabamian" stated that she became a member of the Christian (Church of Christ?) Church under the preaching of Dr. Wharton, and Dr. Abe Ricks advised me that his grandfather, Abraham Ricks was a member of the "Christian Church". And here I shall comment again on the spelling of names. Mrs. Irene Ricks Leggett of Tuscumbia, says her grandfather's sister married a "Meyers" or "Mearers?". Also, Mrs. John P. Ricks of Jackson, Miss. seems to think "Mayers" incorrect. But on the slabs in the old "Mayers" cemetery near where Pheribee Ricks lived, the name is spelled "MAYERS" and not "MEYERS" or "MEARERS". And incidentally this was one of the very early families to settle within the present Colbert County. The grave of James J. Mayers is the second oldest I have ever seen in Colbert County, that of Catherine K. Hooks of Tuscumbia being the oldest. Mr. Mayers died Aug. 7, 1822 aged 50 years. Fannie Winter whom, Abraham Rick's brother, Benjamin Sherrod Ricks married was a daughter of Wm. H. and Catherine Washington Winter who lived in Tuscumbia in the early days. Mr. Winter was wealthy. He and his wife were the parents of twelve children. The youngest, Benjamin R. Winter, was a posthumous child. He married a daughter of Hon. Wm. Cooper. The Winter children, or a part of them, were educated at LaGrange. A number of them moved to Mississippi and were outstanding in that state. Benjamin Sherrod Ricks also removed to Mississippi and a number of his descendants live there now. The Ricks Memorial Library at Yazoo City was established by a daughter-in-law of Benjamin Sherrod Ricks as a memorial to her husband.

Another one of Abraham Rick's brothers lived at Eufaula, Alabama, and he had many other relatives scattered over the country. Col. Benjamin Sherrod, one of the very rich men of Lawrence County, was a near relative of Abraham Ricks.

As has already been pointed out, Abraham Ricks himself was one of the wealthiest men in what is now Colbert County. He is said to have owned about 10,000 acres of land and about 300 slaves valued at from $800 to $1500 each and was one of the principal stockholders of the Tuscumbia Courtland and Decatur Railroad. Mr. Ricks first settled near Courtland at an estate called "Cotton

Garden". He did not live there many years until he removed to the place where he died. There was a small house at the latter place when the Ricks family came. A mansion was completed after a period of about seven years. The place was named "The Oaks". The road from "The Oaks" to the public highway a distance of about 2 miles, was lined on each side by cottonwood trees and was known as *"Ricks Avenue"*.

Mr. Ricks died November 23, 1852 of pneumonia and was buried in the cemetery at LaGrange. A monument made of Italian marble and said to have cost about $5,000 was put to his grave. Many yoke of oxen were required to pull the stone up LaGrange Mountain. On this very elegant monument is the following inscription:

ABRAHAM RICKS
BORN
In Halifax County

North Carolina

October 16, 1791

DIED
November 23, 1852

ROMANS	Chapter I
16. For I am not ashamed of	tion to every one
the Gospel of Christ; for it is	that believeth
the power of God unto Salva-	

The wife of Abraham Ricks is said to have been an unusually lovable character "an angel of mercy" so to speak. One of the longest obituaries was written of her that I have ever seen. I am going to make two or three excerpts from this obituary which was printed in the *"North Alabamian"* (A. H. Keller, editor) for March 26, 1874. The obituary begins as follows: "She has left us, passing from earth as gently and quietly as it was meant, such a gentle spirit should pass away. Fading slowly, as one of earth's fairest full blown roses fade, the roses which she loved so well, and resembled so much. I can see her now, her tall slight form bending over her flowers, inhaling their fragrant breath, her countenance beaming with love to our Heavenly Father who made them all, and full of good will to his creatures from the highest to the humblest.

"How she loved the flowers. Her name is associated with these lovely remnants of Paradise. From the superb Hyacinths and to her early Spring flowers which no where else seemed to bloom in such perfection as for her to the magnificent roses, Cloth of Gold, Lady Augusta, Louvenir de Malmaison, and numerous others which she reared and loved, all will ever remind us of her. And then a Le Marque rose of creamy whiteness, whose large branches once made a bower of loveliness over her front gate, never can I see one without it's recalling memories of her."

"For two generations her name has been the synonym of hospitality in this community. And where has such hospitality ever been excelled? Where was there ever such a genial hostess, with such a delightful home in which to entertain her visitors? How many there are among us who can recall some of their happiest moments, as enjoyed with her. Her lovely home, her flowers, her abundant fruits of the choicest kind, her skill as a housekeeper, which was peerless and the wonderful system and order about her house made a visit to her a truly delightful treat."

"She was truly a ministering angel to her family and friends. Possessing a mind unusually bright, a clear judgement, and a heart that knew no evil. Every virtue found a home in her heart, and made her loved and lovely."

Of the three sons born to Abraham and Charlotte B. Ricks, Wm. F., the oldest, outlived the other two. He was born in North Carolina in 1818 and died at his home about three miles west of Leighton in 1902. He married Ann Elizabeth Allison, a native of Limestone County, who was born in 1831 and died in 1860. He later married a Miss Fields who was a gifted writer and wrote under the pen name of "Aunt Rhoda". She contributed many interesting articles to Mr. McCormick's "*Leighton News*" and I do not know how many other publications she may have written for.

Richard Henry, the second son, was highly educated and a talented musician—especially with the violin. I am advised that the Ricks family as a whole was musically inclined. He is said to have also been a fluent speaker. He was a representative from Franklin County in 1847 and was State senator 1851-52. He died in his 38th year—February 24, 1858.

Abram, the youngest son, married Sallie Pope, a neighbor girl who was well educated and of a fine family. He was born in 1825 in Lawrence County and died in 1878. Three of his children, Mr. Abe Ricks, and Misses Lillian and Birdie Ricks now live at "*The Oaks*".

The ancestral home of the Ricks family was at Brancasler Castle, Norfolk County, England as early as the time of King Henry VIII.

The Ligon family was a prominent one in Franklin and Colbert County affairs. James W. Ligon came to what is now Colbert at an early day—in the 1820's I suppose. He was married to Mary Gannaway in Maury County, Tennessee on Oct. 15, 1818 by Ebenezer Rice, M.G. His son, Abner W. Ligon was born in Tennessee, according to the 1850 census report, and perhaps others of his children. Mr. Ligon was a Justice of peace in the 1830's in Franklin County and served the county as Sheriff before the war. He lived in the "Flatwoods" to the west of Littleville where he owned a large

ABNER LIGON

tract of land. He at one time had a grist mill of Cook's Creek. I remember seeing signs of the mill, or what was said to be it. He was the owner, or part owner, of Ligon's Springs on what is called Ligon Creek. These springs were very popular and were patronized by many people. The waters were analyzed by Michael Tuomey, the State Geologist, in 1851. About 19 years later, Dr. R. T. Abernathy, one of Tuscumbia's leading physicians, had the following to say about Ligon's Springs:

"TO THE PUBLIC

"Mr. Ligon has opened his Springs for the reception of visitors, and having received so much benefit from them during a short stay last Fall, it affords me pleasure to recommend them to the public for all diseases arriving from deranged digestive organs, and especially for diseases of the kidneys.

"There is certainly a very happy combination of free carbonic acid sulphate of iron; chloride of sodium and sulphate of magnesia in the main Spring which rises through a Sand Rock computed to be 150 to 200 feet thick. The Springs are situated in a high, cool, salubrious mountain air and the waters thereof are pleasant to the taste. The Ligons furnish good substantial fare and will bestow kind attention to all whose misfortune may induce them to seek health at their saline fountain, which is doubtless the strongest in the State.

R. T. Abernathy, M. D."

Then in the *"Alabamian and Times"* for August 22, 1872 is the following item: "Ligon's Springs, this season, is crowded with visitors from different parts of the country—Never before was there such a rush for this popular resort. We regret the demand has been greater than could be supplied with accomodations. We are glad to learn new buildings are being erected. Mr. Ligon, the proprietor, is a worthy, clever gentleman and sees well to the comfort of his guests."

The following extract is from Mr. Ligon's obituary published in the *"North Alabamian"* for August 4, 1882. I suppose A. H. Keller was the one who wrote it.

"For a great many years, probably fifty, James W. Ligon's name has been prominently identified with the history of Franklin and Colbert counties, and through all the vicissitudes of their eventful history he has proved himself the faithful servant and fast friend of our people.

"He was a staunch Union man during the war" and etc.

Mrs. Ligon's obituary published in the *"North Alabamian"* for March 9, 1879 and written, I suppose by Mr. Keller, the editor, is as follows:

"DIED

"On the 4th instant, of congestion of the brain, Mrs. Mary Ligon, in the 76th year of her age. She was the wife of James W. Ligon, Esq. to whom she was married in Maury County, Tenn. in 1818. Thus it will be seen that this venerable couple lived together fifty-nine years. For the greater part of her life Mrs. Ligon was an exemplary member of the Baptist Church, and piety and benevolence were the crowning virtues of her long and useful life. Another good Christian woman of a fast fading type has crossed the river. To the aged partner around whose heart stone desolution reigns and to the children who feel the aching void which nothing but a mother's can fill, we offer the heartfelt sympathy which comes alone from one who has tasted the bitter cup and been in the deep waters of like affliction."

(Mr. Keller's mother had died in 1875.)

I really do not know how many children were born to James W. and Mary (Gannaway) Ligon but I do know there were at least five. Their son, Abner W. Ligon, was one of the most prominent men of Colbert County. As is stated in the Womble sketch he is thought of as Colbert's first Probate Judge. He was Judge of Probate through the 1870's at the same time that Wm. Resse Julian was Sheriff. He had previously represented Franklin in the Legislature. Judge Ligon was born May 28, 1821 and died April 25, 1904. He was twice married. His first wife was Rebecca E. Smith, a daughter of James and Nancy (Mullens) Smith of Newburgh in Franklin County. James Smith was one of the most distinguished Methodist ministers in Franklin County. Rebecca E. Smith Ligon was born Oct. 27, 1827 and died May 29, 1888. On her gravestone is written this statement: "She Made Her Home Happy". Judge Ligon's second wife was Mrs. Ida Crawford and a daughter of James A. and Nancy (Martin) Patterson. Mr. Patterson, her father, was a native of Trumbull County, Ohio. He was before the War a wealthy planter, merchant and manufacturer. He lived for a few years at, or near, Decatur; but removed to the neighborhood of Tuscumbia long before the war. Ida Crawford

Ligon was born in 1841 and died in 1908. Judge Ligon died without issue. On his tombstone is written these words: "A just, generous and gentle man. He abides in the peace that passeth all under standing."

From an obituary of him printed in the *"Sheffield Standard"* for Apr. 30, 1904, we are advised that he "had been honored in many ways by the people of his city and county and leaves a record for integrity, honesty and usefulness of which few men could boast". According to this obituary he was Probate Judge 12 years, general county administrator for a number of years, member of the Methodist church for perhaps 50 years and treasurer of the Washington Masonic Lodge for 30 years. I again quote: "No man in this section was more highly esteemed, honored, or revered than Judge Ligon and possibly no man in this community enjoyed a larger acquaintance or more extensive friendship."

Nancy Ligon (1824-1899), daughter of James W. and Mary Ligon, married (1) Thomas Skidmore (1808-1881) for many years a merchant and highly esteemed citizen of Tuscumbia (2) Dr. John S. Napier who had first married a daughter of Aldridge and Ann (Curtis) Myatt. Dr. Napier was a distinguished citizen of old LaGrange and later moved to Waco, Texas where he died in 1889. Prof. John C. Stephenson married a daughter of Dr. Napier. Adline (1826-1882), another daughter of James and Mary Ligon married Asa Cobb, a very wealthy planter of Coahoma County, Mississippi, where he cleared some 1200 acres of land and erected a two story log cabin. His health became bad and as a result he visited Ligon's Springs where he met and fell in love with the young Miss Ligon whom he married in 1845. Twelve children were born to them but only four lived to be grown. Those four included Tom Cobb who fought through the war and "was sent east to school but died his first year in college." Mary Frances married Edward Cammack of Coahoma County; Robert Ligon who was a prominent citizen of Mississippi and Arkansas; and Tomithous who married Dr. Frank Van Eaton also of Coahoma County. A sketch of Mrs. Van Eaton and her family is found in one of the historical publications of Mississippi. Asa Cobb became one of the largest land owners in fertile Coahoma County. He died Nov. 20, 1875 in his seventy-first year. Amelia, a third daughter of James W. and Mary Ligon, was married twice. Her first husband was a Mr. Burton by whom she had several children.

After his death she married Thomas East who had previously married a Miss Sugg. Mr. East was considered one of the wealthiest men in what is now Franklin County. Mrs. Amelia East had a daughter by her first husband named Mary Elizabeth, who married Thomas H. Sugg, a near relative of the first wife of Thomas East. Mr. and Mrs. Thomes H. Sugg were the parents of Mrs. Archie Carmichael, deceased of Tuscumbia and perhaps other children. Mr. Sugg died Sept. 28, 1887 and his widow later married a Mr. Russell. Mrs. Mary Elizabeth Burton Sugg Russell lived until January 9, 1943 dying at the age of 90 years.

Mrs. Amelia Ligon Burton East herself was born Dec. 11, 1831 and died at her home in Tuscumbia Oct. 26, 1911. At the time of her death she was said to be the oldest member of the First Methodist Church at Tuscumbia.

I do not know whom William Ligon, son of James W. and Mary Ligon, married. I believe he removed to Texas, or at least some of his descendants did.

The Ligon family is said to have been closely related in some way to the Cook family who at one time lived at Cook's Bluff which is near Ligon Springs. I have not been able to ascertain how the relationship came about. The mention of Cook's Bluff and Ligon's Springs for some reason has always struck a romantic chord in my heart. Interesting stories have been told about these places and the people who were associated with them. For example, Mrs. Mary Gannaway Ligon is said to have had a pet deer that would venture into the forest and the wild deer would follow it back to the home of its owner. To keep hunters from shooting it she kept a strand of "ribbon" tied on it. The Ligons had among their servants a trusty couple, "Uncle" Mat and "Aunt" Alpha. The latter was an excellent cook. A son of one of my grandmother's sisters married in the early 1870's when my mother was a very little girl. My grand aunt secured "Aunt" Alpha's help in preparing the wedding dinner. It was winter time and a snow fell. For some reason my grandmother couldn't conveniently attend the reception and her sister sent her some of the cake that "Aunt" Alpha had cooked. My mother thought when she saw it with its beautiful white icing that the cake was covered with snow.

There was another well known Ligon family who settled near

Mount Moriah Church in Spring Valley Beat perhaps just after the War. The head of this family was Thomas Henry Ligon (1812-1879) who went from North Carolina to Pickens County, Alabama and later removed to a few miles north of what is now Belgreen in Franklin County where he lived for a number of years. From the latter place he removed to Mount Moriah where his last years were spent. This Mr. Ligon was a successful farmer. He was married three times. He married in North Carolina, a Miss Hocutt by whom he had at least four children. His second wife was Julia A. Barham of Pickens County. She died near Mount Moriah December 14, 1875 and was the mother of two children. Mr. Ligon married for his third wife, Mrs. Mary ("Polly") Boyles who originally was a Miss Cook of the same family of Cooks to whom the James W. Ligon family was said to have been related. And it's interesting to note that P. H. Ligon, son of Thomas Henry and Julia A. (Barham) Ligon, married Adah Boyles, the daughter of his stepmother.

The Hector Atkisson family was one of the highly esteemed ones of the Barton section and its head, Hector Atkisson, was also a native of Amelia County, Virginia, the county of James W. Ligon's nativity. There was also less than a year's difference in the ages of these two men. However, according to Mr. Atkisson's obituary he came to Colbert County at a later date than did Mr. Ligon. The Atkissons came in 1837 so states his obituary. He was a member of the Baptist church for many years and is said to have been a devout man. He was also a magistrate for many years. I believe it is said that Mrs. Atkisson was related to Benjamin Franklin. As already stated she was Sallie Franklin. Her picture shows her to have been an attractive, intelligent woman.

The nine children of Hector and Sallie (Franklin) Atkisson make an interesting study. Eight of the nine were girls. The boy was twice married and had one child by each marriage. Two of the girls never married and they lived much longer than any of their married sisters which I suppose just happened. One of these two, Sallie, died on her birthday—the day she was 80 years old. Of the ones who married three married the same man! I have record of men marrying two sisters, and perhaps of some women marrying two brothers, but this is the only case I recall in Northwestern Alabama of a man marrying three sisters. The man in this case was John E. Donley, member of a pioneer Colbert family.

And it is interesting to know that two of his aunts married the very distinguished, patriotic, rich Greenwood LeFlore of Mississippi for whom the county of LeFlore and its county seat, Greenwood, take their names. But the attraction of the Donleys for the Atkissons or vice versa went still further. Arthur Atkisson's first wife was, as already stated, Susan Donley, and his daughter by his second wife (Lucy Sherrod) also married a Donley.

I have no information on Tilmon A. Whitley (1828-1857) and Robert P. Moore (1843-1902) except that the former was a Mason and the latter was born in Marengo County, Alabama. There is a long obituary of Robert Milton Garner in the *"Alabamian Dispatch"* (John W. Davis, editor) for March 28, 1916, and also an editorial obituary in the same number. From these we learn that Mr. Garner lived about 60 years near Barton and had one of the most valuable farms in that section. He was a kind and charitable man. He possessed a great memory. Shortly before his death he made a complete roster of Co. F. one of the cavalry companies and sent it to Judge John A. Steele at Tuscumbia. But Judge Steele was then at the point of death and never realized Mr. Garner had sent it. The Editor of the *"Aabamian-Dispatch"* stated that Mr. Garner was the oldest subscriber to that paper. He had been a constant subscriber for 61 years. It was on St. Valentine day in 1862 that he and Miss Atkisson were married. Five sons and three daughters were born to them, one son and two daughters were living when their father passed away. The two daughters had never married but remained with their father who lived a widower more than forty years. Mr. Garner himself died March 15, 1916. He was born in Madison County, Alabama December 30, 1832 and was a son of Milton and Sallie Garner. He came to Tuscumbia when he was 16 and lived for several years about 3 miles south of Tuscumbia.

One of the most distinguished men that Colbert County ever had was William Cooper. He was a son of Edmund and Martha (Patsie) Cooper formerly from Virginia, but who later moved to Davidson County, Tennessee. The maiden name of William Cooper's mother was Martha Jackson. William Cooper was born in Brunswick County, Virginia. Following is his obituary (except some verse at the end) which was printed in *"North Alabamian"* for August 19, 1887:

"DIED

at 8 o'clock P.M. on 16th inst. WILLIAM COOPER aged eighty-five years six months and seven days

"Our community mourns the death of its oldest and most distinguished citizen, and the Bar of Alabama probably its oldest and one of its ablest members.

"For three score years he was identified with Tuscumbia, rearing a large family here over whose ____ and interests, although many of them live in different states, he watched with a loving and patriarchal care until he was stricken down a few days ago. Mr. Cooper would have been considered a remarkable man in any age and in any country.

"Of commanding presence, intense purpose, large brain and tireless energy; he has left behind a monument more lasting than the loving hands of his children or the admiration of his friends of two generations can ever build. Casting his lot with the pioneers of the Tennessee Valley when it was yet in the hands of the Red men, without fortune or influence to back him he took the lead in his profession and held it with such men as Ligon, and Hopkins, and McClung, and the Walkers, and Nool (Nooe?), and Townes, and Brickell—legal giants for his competitors. He was rigidly methodical and an unceasing worker. He has probably left a brief of every case he ever undertook and a diary of his every day life covering most of his long and eventful career. As an advocate few men were his equal. His fiery and impetuous eloquence together with his thorough preparation of his cases made his success the rule and failure the rare exception.

"In his family circle he was all that is implied by husband and father. There he was tender, watchful, provident, and loving. He only knew the value of money as it enabled him to provide for those he loved.

"To his children with whom the writer of this was school boy and playmate, he offers a sympathy that springs from the ties of friendship and the most pleasant days spent as a student in their father's office.

"To her who was of himself a part, all hearts in our community go out in deep grief and sorrow."

I have had the pleasure of seeing part of the diary that Mr. Cooper kept, and to me it is truly interesting. It is history "fresh from the griddle". Mr. Cooper was quite an artist and his illustrations added very much to the value of his diary. In recording the death of some friend he would draw a picture of a coffin and other entries were appropriately illustrated. He made notes of the weather, too. For example one summer day in 1881 he wrote "Dry, Dry, Dry". And the summer of 1881 was one of the dryest on record in North Alabama. He infused his diary with bits of humor. I had never thought of Hon. William Cooper possessing such a delightful sense of humor until I saw his diary. I had also thought of him as one who had but little or no religious faith, but Miss Bessie Rather of Tuscumbia, who is his granddaughter, says he was a strong believer in God and was even baptized. However he did not believe in eternal punishment, so I guess he should be classed as a Universalist.

Mr. Cooper's children, as might be expected, married into prominent families. I do not have complete data on all these families but I know the Stoddards, the Shines, the Winters and the Rathers were all families highly esteemed and of much note in Colbert County. John William Cooper's wife was the only child of Capt. and Mrs. John G. Shine who were very wealthy and lived in a famous house near Spring Valley. And William A. Nelson who married Susan McCulloch Cooper was the son of Judge Frederick B. Nelson who lived for many years at Mooresville and Athens in Limestone County. Mr. Wm. A. Nelson was a citizen of Tuscumbia about a quarter of a century and was a most congenial gentleman. He died in Memphis, Tennessee in 1875, aged about 45 years. His brother, Owen O. Nelson was a prominent citizen of Tuscumbia for a long time and I believe represented Franklin in the Legislature about the time of the War.

And before closing these remarks on William Cooper and family, I wish to comment on the fact that he loved his first wife

who is said to have been from Russellville, so much that he named
one of his daughters by his second wife in her honor. Of course
he probably loved the second Mrs. Cooper as well as the first one,
but the incident referred to shows that he did not "forget" his
first wife. His second wife's father, Col. Abner Blocker, was a
wealthy planter who lived near John G. Shine and who came from
Edgefield County, South Carolina.

Mr. Cooper is said to have been chief of the Chickasaw Indians
at one time and they called him *"Oolisk"* due to the fact that he wore
glasses. Indeed a remarkable man was William Cooper!

James A. Stoddard was born in Lichfield County, Connecticut.
His large portrait owned by his granddaughter, Mrs. Russey of Tuscumbia, shows him to have been a very handsome man, of broad intelligence and kindness and firmness of character. And I am advised
that he was a fine character and an elder in the First Presbyterian
church of Tuscumbia. He was a prominent merchant of Tuscumbia.
He and James Throckmorton died within a few days of each other and
the joint comment of them is from the *"Alabamian and Times"* for
March 5, 1874. "The respect which our citizens had for them was
manifested by the large attendance at their funerals. Both had
been residents of our community for a great number of years, and
was highly esteemed by all."

The second wife of Mr. Stoddard and for all I know his first
wife may have been also, was an unusually beautiful woman according to the large painting of her, which is also possessed by
her granddaughter, Mrs. Russey. In 1878 Mrs. Stoddard was married to John D. Inman, another prominent Tuscumbia merchant.
Mr. Inman had been previously married but I do not know who
the first Mrs. Inman was. At the same time that Mrs. Stoddard
was married to Mr. Inman, her daughter, Miss Ellen D. Stoddard,
was married to Mr. Chas. F. Bowen, a son of Wilkerson C. and
Mary E. (Devaney) Bowen, old acquaintances and friends of my
mother's people, Michael Finney, a widely known Baptist minister
of near Tharp Springs, Franklin County, performed the double
rite for mother and daughter.

James Throckmorton owned a steam mill on Wheeler Mountain and was perhaps associated with other business enterprises
and I suppose in farming, too. I find his name linked with that of

Tuscumbia institutions such as being a trustee of Deshlor Institute. I have also seen his portrait which is possessed by his granddaughter, Miss Julia Throckmorton of Tuscumbia. It shows him to have been highly intelligent and suggests that he was of a kindly and perhaps humorous nature. Craig Throckmorton, his eldest son at one time ran a grist mill at Tuscumbia and I believe later ran a saloon—or at least sold liquor and cigars. He moved to Memphis where he lived for many years. Another son, Edmund E. was at one time depot agent in Tuscumbia. Thos. C. another son engaged in farming and lived, I believe at the old homestead.

Throckmorton, in my limited experience, is a rare name. So far as I know, James Throckmorton was the only one of the name to be an ante-bellum citizen of Alabama. His granddaughter, Miss Jylia Goodloe of Tuscumbia, advises me that he was one of a large family of children in New Jersey. There is a Throckmorton County in Texas and its county seat is Throckmorton. The name brings to my mind an interesting occurrence in England during the sixteenth century. In *"The National Geographic Magazine"* for May 1929 is an article by Christopher Marlowe entitled *"A Tour In The English Fenland"*. On page 634 of the *Geographic* Mr. Marlowe says:

"Beyond Ramsey is the quaint old village of Warboys and I recalled a story of witchcraft associated with three women of the village. In 1589 trials for sorcery were common, but none aroused greater interest than of John Samuel, his wife and daughter for bewitching a certain Robert Throckmorton and his family.

"These people lived next door to each other and apparently were on good terms. But one by one the five Throckmorton children cried out that Alice Samuel, John's wife, had bewitched them. They declared that spirit voices continually worried them, and until the witch confessed they would never be better.

"After some time Mother Samuel was lodged in jail at Huntingdon while her daughter, Agnes, was adopted by Mr. Throckmorton for the purpose of ascertaining whether she really was a witch. The children soon fell into worse fits than ever, saying that the girl was responsible. Finally she and her mother and father were brought to trial when the old woman confessed that she had indeed caused the mischief. She was thereupon sentenced to death and executed, as were also her husband and daughter, the two latter protesting their innocence to the end.

"Shortly afterward there was established in Huntingdon an annual sermon on the perils and dangers of witchcraft preached by a member of Queen's College, Cambridge."

Edward H. Newsom, a South Carolinian, settled near Cherokee at an early date and took up a large body of land and erected a frame building with about 8 rooms which burned in 1884. His home was on the public highway and near a famous well known as the "Stage Well". There Mr. Newsom and wife, the former Penelope Rutland, reared a most interesting family. From what I know about some of the descendants, and have heard other people say, I doubt that a more hospitable and congenial family could have been found in all the land. Newsom's Springs owned by Mr. Newsom, or the family, was a lovely place on the mountain between Barton and Frankfort; and was at one time a widely known summer resort.

The sons of Edward H. and Penelope (Rutland) Newsom were distinguished men. Perhaps Charles and John were the two best known. John Newsom was a Captain (and later Major) in the Confederate veteran remarked years ago that, "John Newsom was a fine man". Charles E., or Charley E. Newsom, was a teacher of note, having done most of his professional work in Texas. I find that he conducted a "normal school" in Tuscumbia in 1872. Not only Prof. Newson but also Major John and Millard, who was a mechanic, sought homes in the Lone Star State.

The daughters married men of prominence. I had some acquaintance with J. C. Holesapple. He was a true Southerner, a believer, in white supremacy. Following the War, in which he took an active part, he rode with the KuKluxKlan to help maintain order. I. P. Guy, another son-in-law, was a member of the Guy family who lived some two or three miles west of Tuscumbia and who came from North Carolina. Dr. John Allen Wythe's *History of LaGrange College and Military Academy* contains a picture of I. P. Guy. He and his family lived for many years at Ensley, Alabama. In fact, it appears that every one of Edward H. and Penelope Newson's children, who married, married into prominent and highly respected families.

At Tuscumbia lived the Newsums. There was only one letter's difference in the spelling of the two family names—the Cherokee family used the letter "O" and the Tuscumbia family the letter "U". The two family names were, I suppose, pronounced exactly alike—at least exactly alike by most people. The Tuscumbia Newsums came from Virginia; and some of them, if not all of them, were related to the David Keller family of Tuscumbia. There was Dr. Wm. H. Newsum born in Williamsburg, Va. Dec. 26, 1806 and died February 5, 1862 and Dr. B. F. Newsum, born in "Fluvania" County, Va. Oct. 26, 1815 and died July 27, 1890. St. John's Episcopal Church in Tuscumbia has 3 beautiful stained glass windows as memorials to Dr. Wm. H. Newsum, "founder of the church", William O. Newsum who died of wounds received in the Battle of the Wilderness and Alexander Newsum who died, a victim of the "Great Epidemic" (yellow fever) August 28, 1878. These windows were installed in 1879. There were probably no people in the history of Tuscumbia more highly regarded than the Newsums.

Lydal Bacon Cooper was an outstanding lawyer and highly esteemed citizen of Tuscumbia for many years. Following are extracts from his obituary printed in the *"North Alabamian"* for March 25, 1892. I suppose that Mr. A. H. Keller, the editor, wrote Mr. Cooper's obituary, I quote:

"In the fullness of a well rounded Christian life, in the midst of a large and influential family one of the noblest men we ever knew, and one of the best friends we ever had, passed away last Monday morning. He was a native of Davidson County, Tenn. and came to North Alabama and located in Tuscumbia in 1832.

"As a lawyer few men of our acquaintance ever stood higher especially in Chancery practice. He was more of a judge than an advocate and cared but little for the practice of criminal law. If we ever knew a lawyer to have a high and exalted idea of his duty to his clients and the country one who at the great day of Assize will have no client to reproach him and no judge to rebuke him for attempt to mislead him he was the man. Frank and candid, at times even to bluntness, his sincerity dispelled all harshness, and the wounds he inflicted, if any were only the faithful wounds of a friend."

Mr. Cooper remained active until the end and had strong religious faith. His wife was the daughter of Birt and Harriet C. (Johnston) Harrington who came from Newberry, S. C. about 1828 and settled east of Tuscumbia, where Mr. Harrington was a very successful planter. The children of Lydal Bacon and Frances (Harrington) Cooper made distinguished citizens. Three of the sons served in the Confederate army and all three escaped without a wound, although they were in hot engagements. Two, Samuel J. and William, made outstanding physicians. The former did most of his practice at Tuscumbia and the latter was located at Oklahoma City and married into a pioneer Oklahoma family, originally from New York. The eldest son, Birt Harrington, was a Justice of Peace etc. at Tuscumbia and the youngest of the family, Langstone M. was an operator for the Western Union Company at Springfield, Mo. where he died suddenly in the fall of 1889. Of the two daughters of Lydal B. and Frances (Harrington) Cooper, the elder married one of the most outstanding druggists that Tuscumbia has ever had and the younger married that scholarly and hightoned gentleman, Prof. A. A. McGregor. She is the only one of the Cooper family now living and is one of Tuscumbia's noble women.

Although I believe she never lived in Colbert County, I wish to state that I have ever seen the picture of Patsy Jackson Cooper, the mother of Charles, William and Lydal Cooper of Tuscumbia and the mother of several other children, and the ancestor of many people scattered over the South. She was a very distinguished looking woman reminding me no little of Martha Custis Washington. She evidently was a lady of a very high degree of intelligence, and doubtless of a superb character as her descendants attest.

Charles Womble had the rare distinction of being probate judge of two different counties. He was Probate Judge of Franklin during and after the War, and when Colbert was set up in 1867 he became its Probate Judge. But since the new county was soon abolished and was not reestablished until the last of 18.... or we might say 1870, A. W. Ligon perhaps is usually thought of as the first Probate Judge of Colbert County, and is so listed in Leftwich's "Two Hundred Years at Muscle Shoals". Regarding the personal character of Judge Womble I shall quote the following from the

North Alabamian for June 22, 1876 I suppose it was written by A. H. Keller, the editor.

"Death of Judge Womble

"As we feared on going to press last week, the illness of Judge Womble proved fatal. We believe he was a native of Franklin County and know that he lived in that county at least from early youth. Few men had more friends, and none deserved them more. No man would do more for his friends than he. Kind, unselfish and accomodating, a consistent member of the Baptist church and a good and useful citizen he leaves a large family, who have the sympathy of the entire community in their distress."

Judge Womble's wife is said to have been a fine character. On her tombstone in Oakwood Cemetery at Tuscumbia is this statement: "A Christian, the best mother that ever lived". Of course who ever had the statement put there must have meant it only in a figurative sense for there doubtless have been many other mothers just as good.

It appears that all of Judge Womble's children who married, married into respectful and prominent families. The Reeds and Moodys were old families of Frankfort, the Chisholms were also, I believe, at one time residents of Frankfort and perhaps later of Tuscumbia, the McReynolds and Carters were outstanding families of the Northeastern quarter of Colbert. I do not know whether the Noland family into which James Alexander Womble married were the Franklin County Nolands or not. Miss Ellen V. Page whom Isaac Newton Womble married on December 15, 1872 is of special interest to me personally, for she was my mother's first school teacher. My mother told me that Miss Page was a beautiful young lady with a lovable disposition. I do not know what her father's first name was. He was dead when my mother went to her school and her mother was then married to Cordy S. Badgett of Franklin County. Isaac Newton Womble and his wife emigrated to Mississippi. I was told by Mrs. Mary Louisa Carter that they had a daughter who married a Dr. Ural of that state.

Wm. Amos, Judge Womble's eldest son, lived most of his life in Frankfort, Alabama, which was the home of his parents when his father was Probate Judge of Franklin County. He was a useful citizen and a member of the church of Christ. He and his wife reared a large family. Isaac Newton Womble was Clerk of the Circuit Court of Franklin County, and Chas. A. Womble was Supt. of Education in Colbert County about the beginning of the present century.

I had forgot to say Judge Charles Womble was living in Mississippi when he died. I think he lived near Sardis.

The Oliver Hazard Perry Williams Family of near Cherokee was a prominent one connected by marriage to other prominent families of that section. According to the 1850 Census report Mr. Williams was not a wealthy man, at least not wealthy so far as land was concerned, but he may have become wealthy, I do not know. But I am quite sure that he and his family were highly respected, intelligent and energetic people.

Henry Williams, son of O. H. Perry and Mary (Garrett) Williams was a well known Methodist minister of Cherokee. I believe he was the one to whom Dr. Owen in his *"History of Alabama and Dictionary of Alabama Biography"* referred to as an author. Mrs. Williams' parents, the Carrs, lived at Allsboro. Dr. Charles W. Williams, the second son of O. H. Perry and Mary (Garrett) Williams was a well known physician at Cherokee. James W. the third son was a Civil engineer at Cherokee, and T. Wesley the fourth son, was tax collector and Probate Judge of Colbert. His first wife, Bettie Avery, was a daughter of Capt. Wm. H. and Elizabeth F. (Brook) Avery. Capt. Avery was born in Tuscumbia in 1828 and died at the home of Judge Williams in 1908. He was for many years a steamboat captain on the Tennessee River, and before the War.

Capt. Avery's mother was a Miss Drake and was said to have been related to Sir Francis Drake of the Elizabethan age. It is said that she owned a pet bear when the family lived in Tuscumbia, in its days of its infancy, that was a source of much amusement to the inhabitants. The second Mrs. T. Wesley Willams was from Florence, Alabama.

Of the two daughters of the O. H. Perry Williams family Alice married Charley F. Turner, a Cherokee merchant, who was a son of Wm. Milam Turner and whose wife was a daughter of Dr.

Edward Carter of near Cherokee; and Ida married Willie Harris who was a merchant at Iuka, Mississippi. Mrs. Turner is the only one of the Williams family now living, and is the oldest woman living in Cherokee. But she is as full of life as if she were a young woman. She is truly a lady of a sunny disposition and is the mother of a family of well educated and successful children.

From the different accounts that I have read of William Reese Julian, it appears that if a vote had been taken (as is done in schools etc.) in the 1870's and 1880's to determine the most popular man in Colbert County, very likely he would have been the man chosen. He was born near Moulton, Alabama, but lived in Tuscumbia from early childhood. I understand that his mother's maiden name was Reese. He had brothers and perhaps sisters. One of his brothers went to the far West and after many years returned to visit his relatives in Alabama. The following regarding his visit to Tuscumbia is from the "*North Alabamian*" (A. H. Keller, editor) for April 15, 1881.

"One morning last week as Capt. Julian walked out of the Barber Shop at the Franklin House, a gentleman who was being shaved asked Willis, the barber, if someone had not spoken to the man who had just left, as Capt. Julian. On receiving an affirmative reply, Capt. J. was recalled to welcome his brother who had left here twenty nine years ago, and whom he had never seen since."

This brother of Capt. Wm. Reese Julian was Archie Julian from San Diego, California. And in 1881 San Diego was no little distance. We find that in a few days after the meeting of the Julian brothers in the barbershop, they were on their way to visit a third brother who lived in Tuscaloosa County. William Reese Julian lived a life of rich and varied experiences. He learned to be a printer under Asa Messenger in the old "*North Alabamian*" office and later became a tinner in which he did a successful business before the War.

He enlisted as a Private in Jefferson Davis' regiment in the Mexican War and at the seige of Monterey he and Col. Alex. McClung were the first two men to scale the fortification. He is said to have been a Captain of Artillery and also of Cavalry in the War of Secession. His granddaughter, Mrs. Finley of Tuscumbia says he attained to the rank of Major, but the different accounts that I have seen of him calls him "Captain" Julian, so I am using that same title.

Captain Julian served Colbert two terms as Sheriff having been in that office during the seventies. He was also Postmaster of Tuscumbia in 1875 and perhaps before and after. He was a member of the Presbyterian Church, a most zealous Mason, and a Knight of Pythias. He was a man of varied talents and accomplishments. It was said that he was an excellent billardist, bird shot and Sunday School lecturer. He was a noted deer hunter and was one of a party composed of Capt. A. H. Keller, Dr. R. T. Abernathy, Capt. John S. White, and occasionally of Judge John A. Steele, John E. Donley and E. C. Winston who beginning in October 1865 made an annual 12 weeks hunt to the mountains of Franklin, Marion and Winston counties for several years.

Capt. Julian died of apoplexy. He was buried in Oakwood Cemetery in Tuscumbia. All business houses of Tuscumbia closed for his funeral and the courthouse bell was rung during the time. The funeral procession was the largest seen in Tuscumbia for many years. The writer of Capt. Julian's obituary said he "never knew any one who possessed a kinder or tendered heart than his."

Capt. Julian's wife was Elizabeth M. Croxton, and was of a family who came from South Carolina. Her mother was a widow for a great many years and made her home in the family of Capt. Julian. Also Mrs. Julian had one brother, Dr. B. M. Croxton, "a physician and surgeon, in the Confederate army" who contracted consumption and died, unmarried, in Capt. Julian's home on Sunday July 6, 1873. The obituary of Dr. Croxton states that he was born near Franklin Springs in Franklin County, Alabama (This place is now known as Good Springs and is about three miles north of Russellville). It was said that his only regret at dying was leaving his mother and sisters. His mother died in the home of Capt. Julian in 1876. She was said to have been of excellent Christian character. According to Owen's *"History of Alabama and Dictionary of Alabama Biography"* Mrs. Croxton was a Miss Scott and a cousin of Gen. Winfield Scott. She had three daughters besides Mrs. Julian. Mary and Narcissa married Newletts and lived in Madison County, and Ellen married a Hester and lived in Kentucky.

The children of Capt. and Mrs. Julian who lived to adult life were well known and prominent citizens. Owen Nelson Julian (1854-1932) was a life long resident of Tuscumbia and kept books for Col. W. A. Johnson when a young man. Later he was in the cotton business and conducted a fire insurance business. He was an expert auditor. "A man of keen intellect, sterling integrity, originality in thought and expression, a genial, lovable gentleman was Owen Julian." William Croxton, the third son of Capt. and Mrs. Julian was a member of Co. B. Ala. Inf. in the Spanish American War. He was born in 1857 and died in 1901. Frank N. Julian was, I suppose, by far the best known of the Capt. Julian family. He was secretary of the Alabama Constitutional Convention of 1901, was associated with different newspapers of Tuscumbia and Sheffield and held other positions of honor. During his last years he was connected with the State Department of Commerce (Bureau of Insurance) at Montgomery. Mr. Julian was born in 1872 and died in 1945. He was buried in Oakwood Cemetery at Tuscumbia. In fact Capt. Wm. R. Julian's entire family are buried there.

James H. and Sarah Jane (Coats) Srygley reared a family of children that for intelligence and sterling character was perhaps not surpassed by any other family of Colbert County. Their home was near Rock Creek in the southern part of the county and in what is now called Srygley Beat. The Rock Creek community is now a progressive one with a good church school and other modern conveniences. While there is no postoffice as in former days yet the people gave far better mail service than when there was a Post office. In the days of long ago the people of the Rock Creek neighborhood, as in many other neighborhoods, did not make very much use of the U. S. Mail service as the following extract from Srygley's *"Larimore and His Boys"* will show.

"There was a Post-office at Rock Creek, and the mail came out once a week from Cherokee, a small town on the Memphis and Charleston Railroad. When the office was established after the war no pouch was provided in which to carry the mail. But that was of no consequence. The contract for carrying the mail was awarded to Uncle Jeff Smith, and his overcoat pocket was large enough to hold all the mail on that route with room enough for his gloves and lunch. And in the overcoat pocket he carried that mail regularly once a week for months. What need for a lock and key? Did not everybody know Uncle Jeff? Perish the thought of ever locking anything from him!"

Though the people at Rock Creek did not read many papers and magazines nor write many letters their honesty and confidence in their fellow man is not to be scorned.

James H. Srygley himself was a prominent and useful citizen. He was Justice of Peace and I believe he was perhaps a commissioner of Colbert. He was at one time County Superintendent of Education. He had a brother who was Sheriff of Lawrence County before the war. Col. Saunders said that he "gave satisfaction as high Sheriff of old Lawrence". The Colonel spelled the name "Shrygley" and I have seen the name spelled that way by others. Miss Birdie Srygley advises me that there are three spellings of it —Srygley, Shrygley, Shigley. She also said that the family originated in Srygley County, England and that there is a town named Srygley in southwestern England now. She further says—the family was granted the title squire about the year 1460.

James H. Srygley's father was George Srygley and was a native of Pennsylvania. He was an early settler of Lawrence County living I believe, a number of miles southeast of Moulton. His wife, the mother of James H. Srygley, was Ann Wallace. They reared a large family.

James H. Srygley's wife was a daughter of a Cumberland Presbyterian minister. His name was Benjamin Coates, and it is thought he was of New England stock and of the same family as J. P. Coats of sewing thread fame. Mr. Benjamine Coates wife was Annie Delaney. They both died when Sarah Jane was a child and their several children found homes in different families. This seems to account for Sarah Jane marrying at so early an age.

Mr. and Mrs. James H. Srygley lived at Rock Creek many years, perhaps forty or more. They also had near relatives who lived in that community. Their son, F. D. Srygley, wrote a classic description of that community as it was in the first years the Srygleys lived there. This description is found in Chapter II of "*Larimore and His Boys*". Some of the things he narrated sound almost unbelievable, but he was a man of strict integrity and no doubt told the truth. Of the people he wrote:

"The people were healthy, but poor. They were simple in customs, but honest of heart. They were not highly educated as the world counts education, but they were strong in practical sense and trained by experience and observation in the matter of drawing conclusions from what they saw and heard."

"That was a great country for dogs... To a stranger, so many dogs at church might have seemed out of place; but to those accustomed to their presence, they seemed appropriate enough. A stranger might have even suggested that so many dogs in church would disturb public worship; but those good people could hardly have seen how that could be possible. Who that appreciates preaching, and really wants to hear a good sermon, could be disturbed by a living pyramid of fighting dogs in the open space about the pulpit? Such a thing might attract the attention of frivolous girls and fun-loving boys, but what does a real worshiper care for a dog fight so long as there is no disposition among the owners of the dogs to take up the quarrel? A stuck-up preacher might have felt it necessary to suggest that the dogs be put out of the church but—those people would have wanted to know very promptly what the preacher had to do with their dogs—was he not there to preach the gospel? What right had he to take any part in a dog fight anyhow?"

"In early days they had many preachers in that country. My father was one of the first settlers, and he remembers that there were thirteen preachers in that sparsely settled neighborhood of perhaps twenty families."

"They had camp meetings in those days and such revivals as modern times have never witnessed. The way they could preach and pray and exhort may be inferred from a few facts and incidents gathered from those who were eye witnesses of the glory of those good times of old.

"One of the preachers, being requested to pray for the mourners during a great revival, earnestly, solemnly and seriously besought the Lord to come down and take one of the mourners by the hair of the head, jump across hell and drop him in as a warning to the others."

"One of the preachers who heard experiences before admitting persons into his church, received a young lady upon the statement that she dreamed she was a chicken and saw a hawk high up in the heavens above her. The hawk swooped down to catch her, but she darted through the fence and escaped. The interpretation was clear to the preacher and satisfactory to the church. Evidently the hawk was the devil. The young sister had escaped him by darting into the field of grace, but the escape was a narrow one."

In 1868 there was held a few days protracted meeting at Rock Creek Church House, which had been used by "all" denominations. This meeting was conducted by a young man recently graduated from a Tennessee Baptist College by name of Theophilus Brown Larimore. It was conducted very differently from the kind that I have quoted Mr. Srygley. It was perhaps as effective a meeting as was ever held in Colbert County. The seed sewed there and then is still producing fruit. That meeting had a great bearing on the James H. Srygley family. It was the beginning of a friendship between Mr. Larimore and F. D. Srygley that has been compared to that of "Jonathon and David and Damon and Pythias".

The meeting in 1868 at Rock Creek was the first important meeting held by T. B. Larimore who became one of America's best known and most beloved preachers and who lived until the spring of 1929 when he passed away in California. I do not mean that he was so highly learned or altogether as eloquent as Henry Ward Beecher or DeWitt Talmadge and others of their rank, but I seriously doubt that any of them had a better knowledge of the fundamental facts of the Bible or were beloved by their congregations more than Mr. Larimore. And the qualifications possessed by Larimore were perhaps equally possessed by both F. D. Srygley and F. B. Srygley who graduated under Larrimore at Mars Hill College near Florence, Alabama. Both of these Srygley brothers made very distinguished preachers.

F. D. Srygley was the author of four books—"*Larimore and His Boys*" (based on the work of Larimore at Mars Hill College and his students or "boys") "*Seventy Years in Dixie*", "*Biographies and Sermons*" and "*Letters and Sermons of T. B. Larimore*". H. Leo Boles, a former president of David Lipscomb College, Nashville, Tenn. and a distinguished minister, says: "All of his books are worthy a place in the library of any home." N. B. Hardeman, President of

Freed-Hardeman College, Henderson, Tenn. and one of the most eloquent pulpit speakers of the South says: "I am inclined to think that *"Seventy Years in Dixie"* is worthy of a high place in the literature of the South". Mr. Hardeman means that this book, which is perhaps the best one of the four, is of high literary rank simply from a literary view point.

F. D. (Fletcher Douglass) Srygley died in 1900 in his forty-fourth year. His brother, F. B. (Filo Bunyan) Srygley died in 1940 in his eighty-second year. The latter wrote regularly for the "Gospel Advocate" of Nashville, Tennessee, and compiled a book from the editorials of his brother F. D. Srygley, who was editor of the Gospel Advocate at the time of his death. The book compiled by F. B. Srygley is entitled "The New Testament Church". F. B. Srygley was a "clear and original thinker, a deliberate and forcible speaker, and a free, social commingler with the people."

Of the three other sons of James H. and Sarah Jane Srygley, Felix Grundy, the eldest, was a merchant. He was also a Confederate veteran. Fernando Wallace attended Mars Hill College and took a business course. He was a merchant for several years at Frankfort, Alabama, and later became a lawyer. Floyd Lamar, the youngest of the Srygley brothers, engaged in coal mining.

The four daughters of James H. and Sarah Jane Srygley all married, so far as I know, honorable men. Mrs. Dora J. Hill died in May 1940 the last one of the family.

In conclusion of my remarks on the Srygley family I should state that sometime in the 1880's James H. Srygley sold his home at Rock Creek and he and his family removed to Coal Hill in Johnson County, Arkansas, F. D. Srygley had gone there previously and engaged for some time in the real estate business.

Joshua Burns Moore was a lawyer of high rank and widely known in legal circles over Alabama. It is said that he was reared quite poor although his mother's people, the Burgess family, was rather distinguished for financial standing in Franklin County. His father was William Moore, a soldier of the War of 1812, and his grandfather was Moses Moore, said to have come from South Carolina. William Moore's first wife, the mother of Joshua Burns, died and he married the second time. His second wife survived him many years. I do not know who she was, but she was called "Aunt Sallie" Moore. She drew a pension due to William Moore having been a soldier. J. Burns Moore spent the greater portion of his life at Tuscumbia. He married into the family of Edward Pearsall and therefore was the brother-in-law of General John D. Rather, another very prominent citizen of Tuscumbia. It was on Sunday evening, Nov. 22, 1874, that a tornado struck Tuscumbia and took the lives of some of her best known people including Mrs. Thomas Ella Moore and her little daughters, Nina and Ella Burns. Mr. Moore was out of town at the time of this tragedy. His grief is reflected in the tombstone inscriptions of his loved ones:

"O Ella! dear departed one

Where is thy place of blissful rest"

"Come to me in my dreams precious child"

"Little darling it was hard thus to have lost thee"

The first quotation is on the gravestone of his wife, the second is for Nina who was born Feb. 13, 1867, and the third is for Ella Burns who was born July 10, 1872. Susie Erle Moore born July 21, 1860, and Annie Lee Moore born July 12, 1865, survived the storm and lived for many years, but did not attain to old age. They were both young ladies of a high order of intelligence. Susie Erle was educated at Huntsville. She possessed a voice of much natural sweetness and, I believe, went to Cincinnati to have it trained and for the study of music. She met Dr. John M. Shaller, "a gifted and ambitious young surgeon, a member of the faculty of the Ohio Medical College" and was married to him on Feb. 16, 1887 in New Orleans, Louisiana. In 1887 Annie Lee Moore made a tour of several countries in Europe. It appears that their father was unusually devoted to his family, and after the loss of his wife and two little ones in the great storm, he was perhaps even more attached to his two surviving daughters. Being a very successful lawyer he was able to bestow upon them many gifts and luxuries.

Mrs. Shaller died in 1903 leaving a little boy, and Annie Lee passed away Jan. 18, 1905. Thus ended one of Tuscumbia's most outstanding families—a family that was talented and brilliant, but one that early tasted sorrow and death. The entire family are buried in the same plot in Tuscumbia's Oakwood Cemetery.

Theophilus Coburn was blind for many years and never saw all of his children. Yet he did such work on his farm as pulling fodder quite well. Mr. Coburn's farm was partly on Spring Creek and partly on the mountain nearby. This part of Little Mountain is locally known as "Coburn Mountain". The Coburn family has been probably as good an all round family as Colbert County has had. Theophilus Coburn and his wife as far as I have ever heard, were fine people and reared a fine family of children. They have not been particularly distinguished in any way that I know of, but they have attended to their own affairs and "kept the peace". What a pity there were not more like them!

Theophilus Coburn was related to the distinguished Hogun and McReynolds families of Colbert. Mr. and Mrs. Coburn's children married into highly respected families. They married to a large extent into Franklin County families. The McCullochs, Kirklands, Hoopers, Townsends and Forts were all residents of Franklin. The McCulloch family is one of the oldest and most prominent of Franklin. Elijah McCulloch was the paternal grandfather of the Misses Coburns whom the two Coburn brothers married. He came from Mecklenburg County, North Carolina, and represented Franklin in the legislature. These two Misses McCulloch's mother was Susan Sargent. Her grandfather, Temple Sargent, also represented Franklin in the Legislature. Now, Paul Coburn is Colbert's representative; and he is a great-grandson of Elijah McCulloch and a great-great-grandson of Temple Sargent. He is also a great-great-great-grandson of Major Wm. Russell for whom Russellville and Russell Valley were named. Katie Kirkland, widow of Percy Coburn, is an aunt of Effie Fort, the wife of Maury Coburn. The third wife of Ernest Coburn was the daughter of Dr. Claiborne S. Townsend, an early physician of old Frankfort. The first wife of William Coburn, Miss Barham, was from Pickens County. The Richardsons and Grissoms are from Colbert. I do not know where Mr. James Tubbs is from, but Joel Tubbs, or Tubb, a soldier who fought in the Battle of New Orleans, lived and died near where Jonesboro now is a few miles northwest of Russellville. He and his wife reared a large family. One of their sons, Martin Erles Tubbs, married Martha Johnson of Colbert County and lived in the southern edge of the county. His son, Jack Tubbs, was county surveyor for many years.

THE END.

A similar sketch of Franklin County and its early families will follow in a later issue of this magazine.

THE EDITOR.

COLBERTIANS

By R. L. James

SECTION III

OBITUARIES AND CEMETERY RECORDS

To the Readers of the Alabama Historical Quarterly:

I am releasing another section, No. 3, of my article "Colbertians." I hope it will be possible for me to add one more section but I am sure there will still be many interesting people whom I cannot include. In addition to those to whom I expressed thanks in the preface (See No. 2 Vol. 7) I wish to acknowledge my appreciation to Mr. James Carloss of Elkmont; Mrs. J. F. Craig, Jasper; Mrs. William Malone and Mrs. W. D. Brotherton, Cherokee; Mrs. Emma Scruggs and Miss Mattie Guy, Tuscumbia; and there are probably others who deserve to be mentioned in this connection whom I cannot at this moment recall. Mr. Woodruff Delony gave me quite a bit of information. I was at his house on August 6, 1946, which incidentally, was his eighty-sixth birthday, and had a long conversation with him. Since then this venerable citizen of Leighton, has passed away. He was a son of Dr. Edward B. Delony. I hope to write more about the Delony family in some future issue of the Quarterly.

Sept 4, 1946   R. L. JAMES

I. ISAAC E. YOUNG, OBITUARY

From North Alabamian & Times, March 16, 1871, edited at the time by Joseph Shackelford and F. D. Hodgkins.)

"Our Community was startled Saturday last about 5 o'clock P.M. by the sad intelligence that Isaac E. Young, apparently in the prime of life a few minutes before, was no more; having been suddenly attacked while in conversation with some friends by an apoplectic stroke, and within ten minutes thereafter his immortal spirit took its flight. Never has it been our duty to chronicle so startling an event, or one which threw so sudden a a gloom over this community. We could scarcely realize that he, with whom we had a few minutes before, been in friendly converse, he who was one of our nearest and truest friends, lay before us a silent corpse. Language is inadequate to describe our feelings, and to attempt it would be a mockery.

"ISAAC E. YOUNG was one of the oldest, most enterprising and staunchest citizens of this community, having as early as

1841 settled in this place, and by dint of perseverance and skill in his business, accumulated quite a handsome estate. He was ever ready to extend the hand of charity to a worthy subject and liberally subscribed to every enterprise of a public nature that would be of benefit. To the churches he was liberal in his donations, to his friends he was kind and true, he was ever kind-hearted and liberal to the fullest extent in a proper cause, but abhorred meaness and hypocricy in any shape, and if he had enemies it was from this peculiar characteristic, from his out spoken and frank nature. Isaac E. Young was in the true sense a public benefactor, and as such was appreciated by the good and true; he wished only for that which was rightfully his own, he desired nothing more, and lived in accordance with that sublime and proper rule 'do unto others as you would be done by.' In his death this community has lost one of its best citizens, his wife an affectionate husband, and his friends and the order to which he belonged have sustained a loss which is irreparable. Of his life as a Christian it is not our province to speak, but with Christian charity. we throw a mantle over his foibles, and relying on the dispensation of a wise and merciful Creator, trust that he will be permitted to dwell with the sanctified and redeemed. He was buried Monday at 3 o'clock P.M. The services at his residence were conducted by Rev. B. N. Sawtelle, pastor of the Presbyterian church, in an able and touching manner .... We have never seen so large a concourse attend a funeral in this place, and as an evidence of the estimation in which he was held it is gratifying to us to state that quite a number of the citizens of Florence, together with a large number of the order of Odd Fellows of Florence, came over on a special train and took their place in the funeral procession, and assisted in the services at the grave. The procession moved in the following order: Tuscumbia Cornet Band, Order of Odd Fellows, Hearse, carriages, citizens on foot and on horses. From two until four o'clock P.M. all business houses were closed throughout the city.

"We learn that the Hon. Wm. B. Wood delivered a well-merited and pathetic eulogy on the deceased in the Lodge of Sorrow held by the I. O. O. F. in this place on the occasion, in which he stated he had long known the deceased, who years ago assisted in conferring the degree upon him (the speaker)

"George E. Young, brother of the deceased, organized in 1847, Franklin Lodge, No. 24, I. O. O. F."

Isaac E. Young came from Washington, D. C. and was a carriage maker. Miss Leftwich, in **Two Hundred Years at Muscle Shoals** tells of his making a carriage which won a prize at the county fair in Tuscumbia and was purchased by Mr. Guy of near Tuscumbia who paid $1200 for it. In time of the war, a Federal officer took the carriage from Mr. Guy and had it sent to his home in the North.

Isaac E. Young's wife, Mrs. Priscilla Young, is said to have been a very devout lady. She was, according to her obituary, born in Raleigh, N. C. May 15, 1816 and died in Tuscumbia, April 11, 1883. She came to Tuscumbia from Virginia in 1835 and was married to Mr. Young on Sept. 29, 1842. She was a member of the Presbyterian Church over 45 years.

There was an Andrew V. Young "a native of Washington city" buried in Tuscumbia's Oakwood Cemetery who was born April 5, 1801 and died in Tuscumbia Feb. 19, 1853. His grave is marked with a gun and his dog. I suppose most likely he was Isaac E. Young's brother.

MRS. AMOS JARMAN

II. "IN MEMORIAM"

From North Alabamian & Times, July 3, 1873

"Departed this life at the residence of her son, near Helena, Arkansas, on the 13th of June, 1873, Mrs. Mary Jarman in the 84th year of her age. Mrs. Jarman was born in North Carolina on the 9th of November 1789. She was married to Amos Jarman in that State Oct. 3d 1811, and removed with her husband to Alabama in 1820. They first settled in the neighorhood of Tuscumbia, but removed to Lawrence County; about five miles north of Leighton, where they lived together for nearly forty years. In 1861 she lost her husband, with whom she had lived 50 years. She continued to reside at the old homestead until a few years ago, when she broke up housekeeping and went to live with her children. Mrs. Jarman joined the Baptist Church in North Carolina at an early age and remained a consistent member until her death. For nearly fifty years she was a member of the Mount Pleasant church, near where she lived up to a short time before her death. She was in very good health for one of her age, a few months ago she had a very severe fall, which brought back an old disease of the heart which produced her death. She was laid by the side of her loved companion who had preceded her to the spirit land, in the family burial ground at Mt. Pleasant church. She leaves three sons and two daughters with many grandchildren to mourn her death. In all the relation of life Mrs. Jarman was a model woman. She was a true help meet to her husband in all his labors and trials, helping him by her counsel and prudent cares of things. As a mother she was affectionate and watchful of her children. As a neighbor none were kinder. As a Christian she was consistent and lived out in her daily life what she professed. One after another of the old settlers of this valley are thus dropping off. One by one of our friends are passing over to the other shore. May we who are left behind so live, that when we are called to follow we may have the faith which will enable us, as did our sister, to pass through the dark valley of the shadow of death and fear no evil.

S"

The Jarman home, at that time in Lawrence county, is now in the Town Creek-Triangle. According to his gravestone record, Amos Jarman was born in North Carolina, Nov. 13, 1789 and died Dec. 14, 1861. He was therefore only nine days younger than his wife. Mr. and Mrs. Jarman reared a prominent family of children. The son at whose home Mrs. Jarman died in Arkansas, was an outstanding citizen of that state. There was a daughter, Louisa Ann Jarman, who died in 1848 in her sixteenth year, and who is buried in the family plot at the old Mount Pleasant cemetery. The wife of the late Judge Fox Delony of Colbert, was among the grandchildren of Amos and Mary Jarman.

There were also Jarmans who lived in the old Bethel community. I do not know whether they lived in what is now Colbert, Lawrence, or Franklin county. I also do not know whether they were kin to Amos Jarman or not. In the cemetery at Bethel may be seen the graves of H. Jarman (Oct. 10, 1796—Feb. 22, 1862) and another Jarman who I suppose was his wife, but the first name and the dates are not very clear. It appeared however that she was born June 19, 1798 and died January 14, 1865.

III. HUGH C. LECKEY

"DIED—at Leighton, Ala. on Monday, October 2, 1873, Mr H. C. Leckey.

"His sufferings were protracted and severe. As a business man he had sound judgment, quick perception, remarkable energy and perseverence. He was honest in his dealings with his fellow men, punctual in the payment of his debts, urbane in manner and kind to all. He lived not for himself, but cheerfully dispensed charities to others. Many not connected with him by the bond of relationship received from him great assistance. These acts of generosity will be gratefully remembered. He was a hospitable man; his doors were open to ministers and his friends whose happiness he lived to promote. He had completed a residence, tastefully designed and elegantly executed and furnished, but the hand of death has draped it in mourning. He was a devoted husband and an affectionate brother. May the Lord sustain and console the bereaved.

J. S. Davis

Mr. Leckey's obituary is from the **Alabamian & Times** for Oct. 1873.

Mr. Leckey and his brother, Alexander Leckey, were for a number of years very successful merchants of Leighton. Their store house, which burned in 1911, was at the crossing of the County Line Road and the present Joe Wheeler Highway. Near there was where Hugh Leckey built the residence to which Mr. Davis alluded and which is now occupied by two nieces of his. It was truly an artistic dwelling. Hugh C. Leckey was a native of Ireland. His wife was Ellen S. Galbraith, to whom he was married by the writer of his obituary on January 17,1872. He had a number of brothers besides Alexander, including Thomas Leckey who married a Miss Lightfoot, and a brother who lived in Luka, Mississippi. He had a sister, Jane Leckey, who married first, Samuel J. Leggett and second, Z. Taylor Higdon. I have seen her picture as a young lady, and it shows her to have been quite beautiful and very richly dressed. It is her daughters who live in the H. C. Leckey home and a son of hers, G. W. Leggett was once Sheriff of Colbert County. A grandson of hers, Sam Leggett is the present mayor of Tuscumbia. (August 1946)

IV. S. O. EGGLESTON

"An old and respected citizen died at the residence of his son, W. F. Eggleston, at Bibb's lane, Limestone Co., on last Friday, August 7th inst., was buried at his old homestead near Leighton, Lawrence Co. on last Saturday. He was born in Va. and resided at Tuscumbia for several years. He was nearly 80 years old. For many years was a member of the Christian church, and it can be truly said he was a charitable and honest man. We have known him thirty years, and often enjoyed the hospitalities of himself and excellent wife, for there was no place in this country where the elegant and kind hospitalities of a pleasant home were more liberally dispensed. We cherish his memory."

Mr. Eggleston's obituary is from the editorial page of The **North Alabamian** for Aug. 13, 1874. L. B. Thornton was the editor at the time. Mr. Eggleston would probably be now classed as a member of the Church of Christ. The term "Christian Church" now applies to that denomination that claims to accept the theological views of Alexander Campbell but who use instrumental music in their worship and have the missionary society. Of course, I can not say with certainty what Mr. Eggleston's belief was on these points of doctrine.

His wife died in 1871 and the son, W. F. Eggleston, in the latter years of his life was an outstanding teacher of North Birmingham, Alabama. After he retired from teaching he ran a cigar stand in the Courthouse at Birmingham. W. F. Eggleston first married a Miss Bibb, a granddaughter of Gov. Thomas Bibb. His second wife was a Miss Godley of Tuscumbia. W. F. Eggleston died in December 1913.

In the **North Alabamian** for Dec. 2, 1881, is an obituary, by "A Friend," of John L. Eggleston who died at the residence of Wm. F. Eggleston in Limestone county. According to this obituary John L. Eggleston was born in Hanover County, Va. March 8, 1806 and died Nov. 18,1881. He lived many years in Tuscumbia and vicinity and "was known throughout the valley." The writer of his obituary had known him 40 years. He was also a member of "The Christian Church" and was a very pious gentleman. I suppose that was a brother of S. O. Eggleston.

The wife of the distinguished John L. Townes was Polly Eggleston, a native of Virginia, and was probably nearly related to Samuel O. and John L. Eggleston.

V.

Throughout the world the name of Helen Keller is known. She was born in Tuscumbia, Alabama in 1880, and was the daughter of Hon. Arthur H. and Kate (Adams) Keller. I am very happy to present to the readers of the **Alabama Historical Quarterly** a reproduction of the original obituary of her paternal grandmother

Mrs. DAVID KELLER, and

here it is:

"DIED

In this city on Tuesday the 28 inst. Mrs. Mary F. Keller aged 79 years 8 months and 16 days.

"Mrs. Keller was born in Charles City County, Virginia, near 'Shirley,' on the 12th of January 1796. She was a great-granddaughter of Gov. Spottswood, first colonial Governor of Virginia, and on her mother's side was lineally descended from Lord Delaware. She was also second cousin to Gen. Robert E. Lee.

"With her husband, David Keller, she came to Tuscumbia in the year 1818, and with the exception of two years, which were spent in Russell's Valley, she has lived in Tuscumbia ever since. During this long period no one has been more highly esteemed or occupied a wider sphere in society. All who knew her, or who came in contact with her felt that she was no ordinary woman, and they ever entertained for her the highest respect and regard.

"She raised ten children—seven sons and three daughters—five sons and one daughter are now living and the position which they have taken in society and in the walks of life, speaks eloquently of the influence and training of their now sainted mother.

"Forty-seven years ago Mrs. Keller united with the Presbyterian church, here, under the ministry of the Rev. Ashbridge. During these long years she was an humble, devoted and consistent member, and, at the time of her death was the oldest communicant in the church. Seldom does the death of a good and pious woman cause a greater void in the church and in the society where she dwells.

"Having been faithful in every relation of life, a confiding wife a fond mother, a constant friend, and a true and faithful christian, she was ready for her departure.

"The dying hour found her house set in order, waiting for the summons, and in her case was beautifully illustrated the truth of the scripture promise 'at evening time it shall be light.' Not long before death she said to those around her, 'surely goodness and mercy have followed me all the days of my life' and the light of God's countenance shone up on her to the latest moment of life. Without a struggle or a pang, as gently as the Summer cloud fades away, she fells asleep in Jesus, and her death as well as her life, was a sublime demonstration of the Power and blessedness of the Christian religion.

S"

Mrs. Keller's obituary is from the **North Alabamian** for Sept. 30, 1875. Her husband, David Keller, was a native of Maryland and his father, Caspar Keller, was born in Switzerland, David Keller was very prominently associated with the old Tuscumbia-Decatur Railroad. Perhaps Arthur Henley Keller was the best known in Colbert, of any of the children of Mr. and Mrs. David Keller. He was a lawyer and was appointed U. S. Marshal for the northern district of Alabama by Pres. Cleveland. He was perhaps best known as editor of "The North Alabamian" for a great many years, and to the present generation, as the father of Helen Keller.

Of the Presbyterian minister, Mr. Ashbridge, under whose ministry Mrs. Keller united with the Tuscumbia Presbyterian congregation Col. James E. Saunders said:

"For several years . . . Previous to 1830 a young minister of Tuscumbia, named Ashbridge, occasionally preached in Moulton. He was a man of fine intellect, of high culture, and of a rich imagination. He died early, and his death was very much lamented by people of all denominations. Had he lived to middle life he would have been an orator of the first class."

VI. MRS. W. C. WHEELER

"Obituary

"Mrs. Laura Frances Wheeler, wife of Dr. W. C. Wheeler, and daughter of B. J. and E. S. Smith was born Sept. 22, 1848. and married to her bereft husband Nov. 22, 1866. She professed religion and joined the M. E. Church, South in the autumn of 1867 and died in Cherokee, Ala. Oct. 24, 1876. It is very probable that our sister died without realizing that her sickness was to be fatal, and certainly much earlier than was expected by most of her friends. This being the case, she said nothing on the subject of dying, so far as the writer is advised. She was much beloved by her neighbors because of her uniform kindness to all, and when the tidings spread from house to house, 'Lou Wheeler is dead,' the whole village was in consternation and sorrow. The multitude that attended her funeral attests the esteem in which she was held by all. The writer has been her pastor four years, has lived near her seven, and can testify that in her association she was pleasant and happy. As a daughter, sister and wife she was true and affectionate; and as a mother, she tried to do her duty faithfully. How sad to think three little children are left to make their way through the world without ever knowing the power of a mother's love! How sad the heart, and how desolate the home of my friend and brother who has so often been with me and mine in sickness and distress. May the great Head of the Church soothe his heart with the consolation of his grace! From the life of the deceased we have good hope that with her, sorrow, tears, and trouble, are ended forever. As far as was ever known to me, she was uniform and consistent in her life, and resigned and patient in her afflictions. After such a life we confidently expect the bliss and joy of 'the life to come'   JNO. B. STEVENSON"

Mrs. Wheeler's obituary is from the **North Alabamian** for Dec. 1, 1876.

Her husband, Dr. W. C. Wheeler is said to have been a high class physician and a gentleman of distinguished bearing. He later married a Miss Giles of Tuscumbia; and about 1890 he removed from Cherokee to Huntsville. A sketch of him may be found in **"History of Alabama and Dictionary of Alabama Biography"** by the late Dr. Thomas M. Owen.

The Smiths were among the early and prominent settlers of the Cherokee community.

Mrs. Wheeler's first name is misspelled in her obituary so says her cousin, Miss Mattie Guy of Tuscumbia. It was Louise or Louisa.

VII.   ROBERT A. GOODLOE, SR.

"DIED

At the residence of Wells Rutland Esq. in this county on 8th inst. Hon. Robert A. Goodloe aged 68 years.

"We never knew any one more opposed to eulogy or flattery than was the subject of this notice, and for this reason if there were no other, we shall endeavor to pay a faithful tribute to the best friend we ever had, by writing of him in that spirit of candor and frankness that was so characteristic of him.

"From those now living who were schoolmates of his, we learn that from the earliest boyhood, he was kind and considerated, and earnest and devoted, in his friendship. For the last twenty years we bear testimony to these and other noble traits that rendered his the arts of duplicity or hypocrisy, a candid and blunt manner of speech sometimes offending those who did not thoroughly understand him.

"Mr. Goodloe joined the Methodist church at this place when but fourteen years of age, and for more than half a century remained true to his profession, and died, as he lived, an humble unpretentious trusting Christian.

"During the war when possessed with large means he devoted most of his time to the relief of the hundreds of poor people around him supplying them with food and medicine, and for several years afterwards when his property was swept away and until he was stricken with paralysis in 1875, he continued to do all in his power to relieve the suffering and destitute, and until his last illness was looked up to and consulted by all who knew him as an honest and conscientious counselor, and faithful friend in all kinds of trouble.

"He was many years a member of the commissioner's Court of Franklin and subsequently of Colbert county, bringing to the discharge of the duties of that office, clear and unbiased judgment, incorruptible integrity and a force and vigor of expression that made its impression, and at times conveyed the idea that he was arbitrary and exacting, but the results generally vindicated the tenacity, and stubborness of his opinions. Although endowed with a strong and imperious will and violent prejudices, no one was readier to confess an error and atone for it. Only an intimate acquaintenance such as it was our privilege to enjoy, could impress anyone with the true worth and value of such a men as a citizen or a friend. Whilst we will sadly miss his prudent counsel and his warm and generous sympathy, we yet rejoice that he is freed from every pain and care and has entered upon the full fruition of all the hopes that sustained him through an honorable and well spent life. Our country and the state of Alabama have lost one of their best men—than whom no one in our acquaintance has done more in a private sphere for the good of his fellow men. Peace to the ashes, and a thousand blessings upon the memory of Robert Atlas Goodloe."

The obituary of Mr. Goodloe has no name signed to it. It is taken from the **North Alabamian** for March 17, 1882.

He was a son of David Short Goodloe, an early settler of Tuscumbia, and who was born in Granville County, North Carolina, July 26, 1776, and died Oct. 15, 1845. David Short Goodloe's father was Capt. Robert Goodloe, a Revolutionary soldier, and a native of Carolina County, Virginia, and his mother was Sarah Short.

David Short Goodloe had a family of several sons and a daughter, Sarah Louise Goodloe, who married a man named Kennedy and who died in her nineteenth year. Among his other sons were Albert G. J. Calvin, and Paul. Of these Albert G. Goodloe, born April 13, 1812, died January 1,1887 was said to have been a very devout man. J. Calvin Goodloe, born May 21, 1817, died Feb. 25, 1895 was State Senator from Colbert County (or the district of which Colbert was a part) in 1872-73. He was a strong Republican, but Robert Atlas Goodloe, Sr. was a Democrat.

Paul Goodloe was a citizen of Memphis.

The wife of Robert Atlas Goodloe, Sr. was Mary, a daughter of Col. Isaac Lane who was one of the richest men who settled in the Cherokee district. Col. Lane was from Wake County, North Carolina. There is a long obituary of Mrs. Goodloe in the **North Alabamian & Times** for Oct. 29, 1874. From it we are advised that she was "the last surviving child of Col. Isaac Lane. Reared in luxury and ease, she was plain, elegant and self possessed in her manners, prompt, energetic and methodical in her domestic arrangements. Her charity was only limited by her ability. She was unremitting in her ministrations to the sick, and unremitting in her benefactions to the poor and needy of the surrounding country."

Miss Julia Goodloe of Tuscumbia who is a granddaughter of Robert Atlas and Mary (Lane) Goodloe, has a very large and beautiful painting of two young daughters of her grandparents viz. Sarah Goodloe who married Watt Rutland and Mary Goodloe who married James Mhoon. Each girl was beautiful and the artist, a Mr. Frye, did a most excellent piece of work. Miss Goodloe advised me that the date on the back of the painting is 1858.

VIII.   MRS. ALEXANDER MALONE

"IN MEMORIAM

Mrs. Elizabeth Malone, wife of the late Alexander Malone, died at her home near Cherokee, Ala. Sept. 28, 1884, aged 80 years. She was born in Rockingham County, Va. July 27, 1804. At an early age she moved from her native State to Kentucky, where she lived several years, and from thence came to Tuscumbia, Ala. where she resided a number of years and where she was married to her late husband who died two years since. She then came to the vicinity of Cherokee where she lived up to the time of her death-more than forty-two years.

"While the useful and eventful life of this good noble Christian woman—this mother in Israel—had been spun out beyond her fourscore years, and it might have been expected that at any moment she would be called to reap her rich reward beyond the shining shore, yet, the sorrowful intelligence of her death will moisten many an eye and carry a pang of sorrow to many hearts, for being one of the good women of the earth, none knew her but to praise. A devoted and affectionate wife, a fond loving and indulgent mother and grandmother, a kind neighbor and hearted, true and faithful friend, she endeared to her in the strongest ties, by her beautiful conduct all who enjoyed her acquaintance or the hospitality of her home, where her presence is so severely missed, and where is left a void that none can fill. Her many ennobling characteristics of head and heart shone out resplendent in her daily walks of life, and her many virtues were a fit setting to that Christian character which was so lovely and surrounded by as, a bright halo to the end. She loved her home, she loved her friends and above all, she delighted in the services of that God on whose true and never failing arm she had implicitly leaned for more than sixty-seven years. The sweep of the death angel's wing had no terror for her. Feeling that it was 'not all of life to live, nor all of death to die' she passed peacefully and calmly across the turbid, chill water, and gained the portals of eternal day—the haven of everlasting rest, where the loved ones gone before, and those left behind, emulating her bright example, will meet and strike hands on the banks of sweet deliverance.

W.S.N."

The obituary of Mrs. Malone is from the **North Alabamian** for Oct. 10, 1884.

There is a notice of her death in the same publication for Oct. 3, 1874, written, I suppose, by A. H. Keller. This account says she died on the 27th of September. It says "She belonged to a class of noble christian women who gave character and tone to society in the early days of civilization in the Tennessee Valley."

Mrs. Malone's maiden name was Elizabeth Edwards. She married Isaiah Thatcher and they were among the early residents of Tuscumbia. Mr. Thatcher is buried in Oakwood Cemetery at Tuscumbia as well as some of their children. From his gravestone we learn that he died Aug. 25, 1939 aged 53. There were several Thatcher children. One, who died young, had the very unusual name of "Return." Alexander Malone, the second husband of Elizabeth Edwards, was commonly known as "Sandy Malone." He had been previously married. He was one of the outstanding farmers of the Cherokee section and of considerable wealth. I am advised that Goodloe Warren Malone who also lived near Cherokee, and who was considered one of the wealthiest men in what is now Colbert, and Mitchell Malone a prominent citizen of Lauderdale county were brothers of Alexander or "Sandy" Malone.

Several children were also born to Alexander and Elizabeth (Edwards) Malone and from them have descended respected and well known citizens.

IX. MRS. BERNARD McKIERNAN

"A Remarkable Woman.

A remarkable woman, Mrs. Mary A. McKiernan, died on Friday last, at the residence of her son, Maj. C. B. McKiernan, not far from Florence, Tuscumbia, and Leighton in Colbert County, Ala. Mrs. McKiernan was born in Maryland, March 9, 1792, and her maiden name was Mary Anthony Waters, a sister of Dr. John Waters, an esteemed and wealthy citizen of Nashville many years ago. She came to this city in early life and lived in the family of Dr. Felix Robertson who married her sister, and was married at his residence in 1814 to Bernard McKiernan. Several years after their marriage they removed to Alabama when the country was inhabited by the Indians. Her husband opened a cotton plantation in what is now Colbert county and was a successful planter. He was afterwards a commission merchant in New Orleans, living there in the winter, and spending his summers on his plantation. After the death of her husband she lived with her son, Maj. Charles B. McKiernan. She was the mother of eight children, one of whom was Judge McKiernan of Memphis, who died there many years ago. Two of her sons were buried in the clothes bought for their wedding garments, their deaths occurring before their marriages, two years apart, however. One of her daughters was a noted belle in her day and was married to Gen. Hugh Dunlap of Louisiana. Another daughter was married to W. M. Jackson, of Florence. Mrs. George W. Douigan of this city is a granddaughter of the deceased. All her relatives were highly respectable people.

"The memory of the deceased was wonderful. Ninety-three years of ago, a physical wreck, yet with a mind as vigorous and clear, and her memory as retentive, both as to past and present events, as it was seventy years ago. Scarcely such another case is on record. Only one month before her death her evidence was taken to prove the death of an old citizen of her county who died sixty years ago. She gave the history of the family, the names of the children, to whom they were married, when the old man died and where buried, with as much minuteness as though it had occurred at a recent date. She signed her name plainly to the deposition, and the attorney said it was the most remarkable case he had ever witnessed.

"Her burial took place Sunday last, at 11 o'clock, in the presence of many relatives and friends and a number of her old servants all whom were devotedly attached to the good old woman. She passed away to the spirit land calmly, peacefully, quietly. She rests from her labors and her works will follow her. A very large circle of relatives and friends in Alabama, Tennessee and other States will mourn the departure of this aged Saint."

Mrs. McKiernan's obituary is from **Nashville-American** in the **North Alabamian** for Feb. 13, 1885.

The **North Alabamian** for June 24, 1881 records a visit of Mrs. McKiernan to Tuscumbia. The account said that she was suffering from a fall of recent date but that she was still cheerful. It also stated that she had always been fond of the society of young people and that she had been noted for hospitality.

There was a David C. Waters who died at the residence of Mrs. Sarah C. Hogan near Tuscumbia. Jan. 25, 1873. He was born in Anne Arundel County, Maryland, February 22, 1794. He moved to Nashville, Tenn., in 1812 and was a merchant there for several years. He then came to the vicinity of Tuscumbia. He is said to have been a very amiable gentleman and was polite to the nth degree, I am not advised whether he was related to Mrs. McKiernan or not, but I am inclined to believe he was.

X. GEORGE GEISE

OBITUARY

Bro. George Geise was born in Lancaster County, Pa. March 27th, 1810 and died September 14, 1892, at his home near Dickson, Ala. He moved from Pennsylvania to Tuscumbia, Ala. in 1839 and was married in this place in 1839 to Miss Martha Ann Steger. It was a congenial, happy union of hearts and hands. In 1859 he moved to Mississippi, and returned to Colbert County in 1868? After a protracted illness brought on by a stroke of paralysis, Uncle George submissively yielded his sanctified spirit unto the beneficent hands of his Lord and Master, surrounded by loved and loving ones, together with kind friends who appreciated his true moral worth, his uncompromising integrity. He was one of God's noblemen. His fond, trusted and cherished companion, Martha Ann, was a good woman, a true friend, an exceptionable Christian. She passed away in November, 1889 in the blessed hope of the Redeemed. Both husband and wife were devoted acceptable and honored members of the M. E. Church, South. They had born to them six children—five sons and one daughter—all now living except Henry who died at his parents home in February in 1890. Those who knew Uncle George best, loved him best. He was ever true to his trust as the needle to the Pole. His moral character was above suspicion as guileless as a child. His hospitality, benevolence and charity scarcely knew any bounds. His household was one of industry, harmony and peace. He was true to his God, family, friends and country. He was called from his happy earthly home to join the mother and loved ones, gone before to the saint's eternal rest in Heaven. May the irreparable loss prove to the dear children a present and eternal blessing.

"Farewell, Bro. George, for a short season.

F. A. Ross."

To obituary of Mr. Geise is in the **North Alabamian** for Sept. 30, 1892.

There is an article in the **North Alabamian** for Oct. 3, 1890, telling about Mr. Geise being in Tuscumbia "today". From this we learn that he was the oldest surviving engineer who ran a locomotive on the Tuscumbia and Decatur Railroad, except Capt. Jack Lawson of Paducah, Kentucky. Mr. Geise, according to this account, made the first trip in June, 1837, using pineknots for fuel. He was later transferred to the shops where he worked several years. He then went into business for himself and made a fortune. He was very active in October, 1890. Mr. Ross stated he came to Alabama in 1839 (if not the printer's mistake) but this account states he was on the Tuscumbia-Decatur Railroad in 1837.

Another well known citizen of Tuscumbia was Reuben Geise also from Pennsylvania. I have not been able to ascertain whether he and George Geise were brothers or not, but most likely they were. Reuben Geise was in the milling business at Tuscumbia for many years and once had Gov. Lewis associated with him, so stated a local historian. The mill was long known as "Geise's Mill." Later Mr. Hindman, another Pennsylvania, became owner of the mill, and it was "Hindman's Mill" for many years.

XI. J. M. HUSTON

"DIED

In this city, on the 23rd ult. of heart disease, Dr. J. M. Huston of Dickson, Ala.

"The deceased was born at Harrisonburg, Va. February 3rd, 1826, graduated at the Philadelphia Medical College and came to Buzzard Roost, Ala. in 1851 to practice his profession. In 1857, he married Miss Annie Barton, daughter of Armistead and Amanda Barton, and to them were born seven children, all of whom are alive except one son. Dr. Huston practiced his profession at Dickson until a few months before his death. His malady commencing to show alarming symptons and medical attention being difficult to procure at his old home, he was moved to

Tuscumbia the home of his son-in-law, Dr. C. R. Palmer, where he might receive the benefit of his attention. He gradually grew worse until the morning of the 23rd when he breathed his last, without pain or struggle. He was a member of the M. E. Church and died with a firmly founded hope of eternal life. He was buried at the Barton burying ground just as the sun was setting Friday the 24th attended by a large concourse of grief stricken relatives and friends.

His place will be hard to fill at his old home, as he had a warm place in the hearts of all. He was a FRIEND as well as medical advisor to the whole country for miles around. These ties were moulded all the closer by his many acts of charity and kindness. He was prepared to go when his Master said, 'Come up higher' and gladly laid his hand in the hand of Christ and quietly went to inhabit the mansions in the skies.

A FRIEND"

Dr. Huston's obituary is from the **North Alabamian** for March 3, 1893.

There were also HOUSTONS in the early settlement of Colbert and some of their descendants are still to be found in the county. I do not have any information as to their ancestry of family connection. But from looking through old newspaper files I find two interesting references to men whose name was spelled HOUSTON.

It was said that James Houston killed a 200 pound deer within two miles of Tuscumbia in December 1872. Then the **North Alabamian for** June 30, 1882, records the death of Dr. N. J. Houston at San Antonio, Texas. The paper states that Dr. Houston was a citizen of Tuscumbia for more than forty years.

XII. MRS. WM. B. ALEXANDER

"IN MEMORIAM

Mary E. Alexander was born unto A. and Mary Jane Avery April 21st, 1834, and died at her home in Cherokee, Colbert County, Alabama, on May 24th, 1894, aged 61 years, 1 month and 3 days (60 years, is correct, instead of 61). Having returned from a short visit to see her daughter, Mrs. Erwin in Texas, she was taken seriously ill in two days after her arrival and passed away within eleven hours.

"Sister Alexander was married to Bro. W. B. Alexander, December 20, 1853. As a result of this union eight children were born, five of whom survive to cheer and comfort the father in his afflictions. Sister Alexander joined the Methodist church at Driskell's Chapel in Lauderdale County, Alabama, and remained an unassuming, consistent member until her death. She was very modest and reserved yet, she was classed with the most faithful in her church. Possesed of superior industry and economy, she was a literal success financially. The heavenly blessings were richly upon her labors. Indeed she managed her affairs with much discretion. She had the confidence and esteem and friends and patrons. Her aim in life seemed to have been to make home the center of attraction for her children, and in this, success crowned her efforts. She was ever ready to respond to the calls of true charity and to support the institutions of her church. The writer of this never visited her home, if at all convenient, but that he was called upon to read the Scriptures and lead in prayer with the family. Those who knew her best loved her most. She is gone, yes, gone but not forgotten. 'Blessed are the dead which die in the Lord: they shall rest from their labors and their works do follow them."

A. J. Maddox"

Cherokee, Ala. Aug. 26,)'94

(Will the **Florence Times** please copy?)"

Mrs. Alexander's obituary is from the **North Alabamian** for Aug. 31, 1894.

Mrs. Alexander was a sister of Capt. Wm. Avery whom I have mentioned in connection with the O. H. Perry Williams family. She had other brothers and sisters, one being Mrs. Fannie E. Bell (1826-1901) wife of James Porter Bell (1818-1872) of Cherokee.

The husband, Wm. B. Alexander, was born Dec. 3, 1827 and died Sept. 19, 1906. He is said to have been of sterling character. Mr. Alexander, according to the account in the Tuscumbia Dispatch" for Sept. 22, 1906, left the following children: Mrs. (Dr.) C. W. Williams of Cherokee, at whose home he died; one son, Dr. J. F. Alexander of Blockton, Ala; and three other daughters, Mrs. Robert G. Malone of Arkansas; Mrs. W. G. Erwin of Texas; and Mrs. G. D. Hall of Iuka, Mississippi.

Many interesting records are to be found in the old cemeteries of Colbert (the same is doubtless true of every other Alabama county). I have not visited all the old ones of Colbert, but I do have records from quite a number of public and family burial grounds. The largest, of course, is Tuscumbia's Oakwood Cemetery unles we include Sheffield's Oakwood Cemetery, but the latter cemetery contains very few old graves. From an interesting history of Tuscumbia, published in the **Tuscumbia Democrat** in 1881 and 1882 by "H" we are advised that the first person buried in Tuscumbia's Oakwood Cemetery was a young man, whose name was Warren and who died near Tuscumbia in the summer of 1817 or 1818. Mr. "H" says that he was buried at night due to the warm weather hasting decomposition of the body. Of course there was no such thing there and then as embalming a human body. Also there was not enough lumber in the new village to make a coffin, so two young men were sent to Fuque's sawmill several miles away to get lumber to make it, and all of this required time.

According to Leftwich's **Two Hundred Years at Muscle Shoals**, the oldest marked grave in this cemetery is that of Mrs. Catherine Kenan Hooks, wife of Curtis Hooks, who was born according to the marker, Sept. 11, 1779 and died Oct. 24, 1821. Curtis Hooks, her husband, was born Nov. 30, 1788 and died May 28, 1848. He was therefore much younger than Mrs. Hooks. According to local history he was a "ranger."

The second oldest marked grave in this cemetery of which I have record is that of Nancy E. White who was born Dec. 16,

1781 and died March 2, 1882-just a little more than four months after Mrs. Hooks died. And a third marked grave for the year 1822 is that of a little girl who died when nearly four years of age at an age when a child is the obpect of such parental devotion as to call to mind Eugene Field's immortal poem, **Little Boy Blue**. This grave has a coffin-shaped tablet with the following inscription:

> Beneath this Stone
>
> lieth the remains
>
> of
>
> MARGARET FOWLER MITCHELL
>
> born 14 January 1819
>
> died 6 December 1822

One large monument has eight inscriptions on it. They are: Susan McClung Jan. 20, 1812-Sept. 10, 1832; John A. McClung died Sept. 13, 1832; Calphurnia C. Keenon, Dec. 23, 1807-Hay 31, 1833; James Y. McClung Sept. 3, 1831-Sept. 1, 1833; Y. A. Gray, April 13, 1786- Feb. 12, 1834; Martha W. Gray, June 11, 1829-Sept. 1834; Robert H. Gray Sept. 9, 1833-July 3, 1835 and Elizabeth F. Gray, July 30, 1823-Aug. 1844.

There is an old slab near this monument which has Y. A. Gray's name and birth and death dates. On the slab his name is given as "Dr. Young A. Gray." Saunders in writing of the early history of Courtland, Alabama mentions "Dr. Young A. Gray" as one of the doctors in htat town.

Near one of the entrances to the cemetery can be seen the markers to the graves of the Frederick D. Hodgkins family whose lives were wiped out by the great storm of Nov. 22, 1874. On Mr. Hodgkins' gravestone is the following inscription:

> FREDERICK D. HODGKINS
> Born in
> Oxfordshire, England
> Nov. 26, 1842- Father, Mother,
> Four children killed by the
> storm which visited Tuscumbia
> Nov. 22, 1874

Mrs. Hodgkins was a daughter of James and F. Carter and was born in Bedford County, Tennessee Feb. 12, 1846. F. D. Hodgkin was a jeweler by trade and was also an editor. St. Johns Episcopal Church at Tuscumbia has an interesting stained window dedicated to the memory of the Frederick D. Hodgkins family.

Following are two reproduced inscriptions from this cemetery:

In Memory of
ROBERT B. MALONE
BORN
January 11th, 1795
DIED
May 21st, 1830

Reader remember as you now are,
So once was he,
As he now is,
So you must shortly be.

I am advised that he was the father of John Lewis Malone (1827-1908) who married a daughter of Armistead Barton and was wealthy. Robert B. Malone's wife was Eliza Minerva Brown.

JAMES DESHLER
A Brig. Gen. Confederate Army
BORN
at Tuscumbia Feb. 18, 1833
FELL AT THE BATTLE OF CHICKAMAUGA
Sept. 20, 1863
Aged 30 years 7 months 2 Days

Gen. Deshler's father, Major David Deshler, was one of the most prominent citizens Tuscumbia ever had. He was born in Lehigh County, Pennsylvania, Sept. 10, 1798 and died at Tuscumbia Dec. 6, 1871. The writer of his obituary said that he had resided at Tuscumbia more than forty years. Among the things he wrote about Major Deshler was this:

"Maj. David Deshler was no ordinary man; of strong natural abilities, a close penetrating mind, cool clear judgement, and of good education, there was scarcely any subject within the range of human thought or speculation he had not investigated. No one within the writer's knowledge had a more comprehensive store of general information on so great a variety of subjects. He is identified with the early history of the State, and was the Pioneer in the South of that great system of railways which now add so much to the wealth and prosperity of the entire country. Under his supervision and mainly through his instrumentality the first railroad in Alabama was constructed from Tuscumbia to Decatur.

"Charity with him was a principal, to the needy he was never known to turn a deaf ear, or to refuse his sympathy and aid to the suffering humanity."

All through life Maj. Deshler was a man of action. Shortly before he died he made a trip to Philadelphia. He had no relatives in Colbert county when he died, at least on close relatives. Mrs. Deshler had died in 1854 and later his oldest son died suddenly while a pupil at West Point Academy, and last his son, James, was killed at Chickamauge. Maj. Deshler gave the grounds and building of the old Deshler Female Institute to Tuscumbia as a memorial to his son. Gen. James Deshler. The Deshler High School at Tuscumbia helps to perpetuate his memory.

Among other gravestone inscriptions in Tuscumbia's Oakwood Cemetery of persons who died before 1875 are the following:

Isabella Elliot, wife of James Elliott, born in Edinburgh, April 13, 1809, died Dec. 8, 1825; Eliza H. wife of Peter Walker, born in Bedford Co. Va. died June 20, 1834; John Sutherland, Sr., born in Pittsylvania Co. Va. July 19, 1752 died Sept. 7, 1836; Peter Walker, born in Amherst Vo. Va. died July 24, 1844 aged 51 years, 2 months and 18 days; Catherine, daughter of Peter and Peter and Eliza Walker and wife of Thomas Mattingly, born in Amherst Co. Va. March 29, 1823, died in Lawrence Co. Ala.

Oct. 1849; Hugh Stephens, born in Donegal, Ireland died 1856 aged 85 years; James Conner, born in Halifax Co. Va. Mar. 9, 1795 died April 7, 1857; "Mary Ann-consort of Lewis Wood dec'd-Born in the City of Richmond, Va.-died in Tuscumbia, Ala. Sept. 8, 1857 aged 53 years"; William C., son of Abner B. and Julia A. Blocker, born Oct. 4, 1845 a member of Co. C. 11 Regt. Ala. Cavalry was killed in action at Pulaski, Tenn. Sept. 27, 1861; Elizabeth G. Kidd Ottaway, born in Fluvania Co. Va. Dec. 5, 1806 died in Tuscumbia, Ala. Mar. 28, 1862 "Love, kindness and Christianity marked her daily walk"; J. E. Johnson, "a Confederate soldier and military prisoner at Rock Island" born March 4, 1839 died March 4, 1864; Major Dick Johnson, C. S. A., born Oct. 18, 1831 "wounded on the battlefield" died July 9, 1864; Elizabeth, wife of Alexander Ross, born in Spotsylvania Co. Va; Sept. 15, 1788 died April 26, 1867; B. Gledall, born in London March 18, 1794 died Au. 13, 1868.

Sometimes dates are wrong on tombstones. John Fletcher Pride, the grand old man, who lived to be almost one hundred years old is buried in Oakwood. He was born near Raleigh, N. C. Aug. 26, 1791 and died near Pride Station, Colbert, June 15, 1891. But the incription on the Pride monument in Oakwood says he died June 15, 1892.

Then there is the case of James Young who lived on Spring Creek near old Hunter. The monument to Mr. Young's Grave says he died February 29, 1815! Of course February in 1815 had only 28 days.

The cemetery at old LaGrange contains some very interesting incriptions. I have already spoken of the very elegant and expensive monument to Abraham Ricks. There are several other monuments that contain far more data than the Ricks monument. For example the elegant monument at the grave of Mrs. Eliza Jane Harrington is very rich in sentimental inscription. She was the daughter of James F. and Susan E. Reilly and the wife of Wm. H. Harrington. She was born March 10, 1817 and died June 21, 1855. Some of the other interesting markers are those to Patience A. W. wife of Thos. E. Tartt, who died Jan. 1, 1837 aged 44 years, 2 months and 15 days; Prof. James M. Hardy born in Lincoln Co. Ga Jane 19, 1815 and died Aug. 5, 1853; Mrs. Susan Adelaide Williams, wife of Prof. Wm. G. Williams and daughter of Capt. R. R. and Mrs. J. S. Miller "late of Richmond, Va." born in Manchester, Va. Dec. 12, 1818 died Feb. 2, 1859, and Laura L., wife of John Moore "who departed to be with the angels" on Sept. 2, 1875.

Among some of the most distinguished people buried at LaGrange are Prof. Hardy, the third President of LaGrange College and a Methodist minister of note; Amanda, the second wife of Bishop Paine; Ann Eliza, the first wife of Dr. Edward Wadsworth and only daughter of J. B. and Elizabeth Felton, the latter who was a sister of Gov. Swain of North Carolina; the Ricks family; Munroe Fort; Dr. George E. Kumpe and wife; Dr. Sidney Smith Prince (1804-1831); Tignal Jones; Martha Burchet Jones; H. K. Felton; Daniel Spangler; Henry Warren; H. P. Looney; Silas M. Fowler; Mrs. J. S. Hawkins; and Mrs. Virginia Hobgood.

Following are some inscriptions reproduced from old LaGrange cemetery:

SACRED
to the memory of
PHILIP PENLETON BARBOUR
The lovely and interesting son of
THOS. S. & S. B. BARBOUR
who departed this life
April 6, 1837
Aged 3 years 7 months
and 15 days

Death's gloomy portals he has crossed
and safely reached the Peaceful shore
no more upon the ocean tossed
The haven's gained the crown secure
For tis of such that Jesus said,
"Suffer them to come to me"
And though to his fond parents dead
Saviour, he lives with thee.

The little Barbour boy's father was a professor in LaGrange College and was a son of Hon. Philip S. Barbour, M. C.

of Virginia. Dr. Barbour left LaGrange and became a professor in the St. Louis medical college.

   In Memory
      of
   Amanda Malvina Paine
consort of Robert Paine
   Her life exemplified the lovelin
   ess of woman her death the triu
   mph of the Christian
      Born July 29, 1813
      Died Sept. 18, 1838

Prof. McGregor in his **History of LaGrange College** says that she was the daughter of a Presbyterian minister by name of Shaw who lived at Columbia, Tennessee and that she was Bishop Paine's second wife. I do not know who his first wife was. His third wife was Mary Eliza Millwater, a daughter of Mrs. Millwater nee Weeden, of Baltimore who became the second wife of Turner Saunders, one of the founders of LaGrande College. Bishop Paine was a very scholarly gentleman and of much executive ability. LaGrange flourished under his administration. He finally located in Aberdeen, Mississippi and died in 1889? His stepfather-in-law, Mr. Saunders, who was also a distinguished Methodist preacher, spent his last years at Aberdeen.

      Memento mori
      SACRED
      TO THE MEMORY OF
      WILLIAM D. DALE
      BORN IN WASHINGTON COUNTY, ALA.
      DEC. 5, 1828
      DIED Feb 28, 1846
      Aged 17 YEARS 2 MONTHS
      And 28 DAYS
Early bright and chaste as morning dew
He sparkled, was exalted and went to heaven
      N. E. C. S. G. A.

1859

ALICE

Aged 2½ years

Daughter of

JOHN C. and MARY C.

STEPHENSON

"Little Alice was our darling
Pride of all the hearts at home
But the angels up in Heaven
Gently whispered; Alice come"

The father of Little Alice Stephenson, Prof. John Calvin Stephenson was reared at, or near Mount Hope, Lawrence County, Alabama. He graduated at LaGrange College and became a professor in that institution. As I have already said, he married a daughter of Dr. John S. Napier of LaGrange. The Napiers and Prof. Stephenson finally went to Waco, Texas. It seems that Prof. Stephenson always had a great love for old LaGrange and vicinity. He is said to have possessed an unusually fine memory and no doubt was a man of superior intelligence. He made many contributions to **The Leighton News** published many years ago by the McCormacks at Leighton.

A few miles east of LaGrange in the Town Creek-Triange, in a small cemetery containing the graves of Alridge Myatt and wife, Col. Richard Prewit, J. R. Bates, Sallie P. Bates, and others. I do not have any data on J. R. Bates, but his tombstone shows that he was a mason and that he was born Jan. 10, 1816 and died Feb. 24, 1867. Col. Richard Prewit was widely known as a man of excellent business judgement and of great energy. Woodruff Delony tells me he had very little literary education, but was a man of very fine intelligence. Col. Saunders in **Early Settlers of Alabama** writes of the Prewits in the early days of Lawrence County. Col. Saunders says the following of Richard Prewit:

"Richard lives near Leighton, and carries with him all the bold characteristics I have mentioned as belonging to his race. When I first knew him he lived on a plantation five miles Northeast of Moulton, well stocked with slaves and mules, and it had the highest fence I ever saw. Moreover, there was a splendid pack of hounds showing that he wisely understood the art of mingling labor and amusement. But he was seized with the ambition of being the largest planter in the county, and I think he became so, for he had some 1500 acres in cotton, when, unluckily, the war broke out, and he was crippled in his estate; but he still has enough, and I judge he is a happier man than he was before. He first married a daughter of Senator Fleming Hodges. The name of his second wife I am not advised of.

The above excerpt from **Early Settlers of Alabama** was written about 1880 or 1881. Col. Prewit according to his gravestone died on November 23, 1882. He had been a resident of the Town Creek Triangle for a number of years. The date of his birth is given as being Sept. 19, 1809.

Col. Saunders states that the first Prewits he knew of came from Clinch River in east Tennessee to Madison County, Alabama. The head of the family lived to be 112 years old and his wife attained 116 years of age!

In the same cemetery in which Col. Richard Prewit is buried are buried descendants of his, and on the gravestones their names are spelled "Pruet".

It appears that the younger generation do not spell it as did the older ones.

And here are the reproductions of the records for Mr. and Mrs. Aldridge Myatt:

In Memory
of
Aldridge Myatt
Born
Feb. 24, 1780
in Wake Ct'y, N. Carolina
Died
Oct. 8th, 1850
He lived
more than 30 years
an exemplary
member
of the M. E. Church

and died in the triumph
of Faith
Let me die the death of
the righteous, and
let my last end
be like his.

Sacred
To
the memory
of
Mrs. Ann Myatt
wife of
Aldridge Myatt
who was
born Jan. 7th, 1788
in Wake Ct'y, N. C., was
member of the
M. E. Church
lived
a devoted
Christian and
departed this life
the 19th July 1840
in the 53 year
of her age
In full
confidence
of a glorious
immortality

Mrs. Myatt was one of the noted four Curtis sisters, the others being Mrs. Hartwell King, Sr., Mrs. John Rand and Mrs. Drury Vinson. All four sisters and their families came to what is now Colbert in 1826. Dr. John S. Napier's first wife was a daughter of Mr. and Mrs. Aldridge Myatt. Therefore little Alice Stephenson, who is buried at old LaGrange was their grandchild.

The following is from the Hampton cemetery northeast of Leighton in the Town Creek-Triangle.

> In memory of
> Cynthia Hampton
> Daughter of
> Andrew & Sarah Mitchell
> Born in Ioredell County, N. C.
> June 24th, 1795
> married M. B. Hampton
> the 28th of February 1822
> Departed this life at
> Murfreesboro, Tenn.
> the 21st of May 1853
> She lived and Died a Christian and was
> beloved by all who knew her
> M. B. H.

Mrs. Hampton's husband, Monoah Bostic Hampton, was born, so states his tombtone, in Stoke County, N. C. June 25, 1799 and died Feb. 16, 1858. He was therefore four years younger than Mrs. Hampton. The reader will notice that their birthdays were in consecutive order. Mr. Hampton was a large planter and his children had fine opportunities for an education. In the family cemetery is the grave of Cynthia Amanda Hampton who died at school in Athens, Ala. on Sept. 28, 1843 in her seventeenth year. M. B. Hampton, Jr. attended LaGrange College but did not graduate. He lived at the old homestead and was said to have been a scientific farmer. I believe there was one son who was prominent physician of Madison County, and there were several daughters one who married Dr. Wm. Parbury or Parberry. Dr. Parbury was a native of Kentucky but was reared in Cole and Pettus Counties, Missouri. He was a successful physician but the last years of his life were devoted mainly to sheep raising in Montana.

In the cemeteries at old Brick and Mt. Pleasant are to be found the names of Carlock, Harrison, Alexander, Carter, Letsinger, Hughes, Craig, Karg, Davison, Gillean, Morrow, Hooks, Hall, Wingo, and others but I wish to call special attention to the three other cemeteries and then I shall bring Section III to a close.

Some three or four miles southwest of Tuscumbia is a small cemetery where M. C. Byrd, Mrs. Byrd, and a number of their descendants are buried. This cemetery is near the home of Cicero Byrd who is a grandson of Michael C. Byrd. James Byrd, son of Michael C. and father of Cicero, reared his family there, and others of the Byrd family lived nearby. Ten children were born to Michael C. Byrd and wife. Mrs. Byrd before her marriage was E. J. Donley, a member of the well known Donley family of whom I spoke in connection with the Hector Atkisson family. M. C. Byrd was one of the first Superintendents of Education that Colbert had, perhaps he was the first. In 1874 he was a candidate for Sheriff of the county but he took sick and died on the 9th of September, so says his gravestone record. Mrs. Michael C. Byrd, who was born Nov. 16, 1832, lived until August 26, 1909.

But the most interesting record in this cemetery is not to be found on the Byrd markers, but on that of a young man whose name was Patrick H. Sheffield. And here is the reproduction:

> In memory
> of
> Patrick H. Sheffield
> Born Sept. 12th, 1813. Died
> Decr. 6th, 1834 for want of
> Skill in a pretended physician
> Then basely slandered
> By the quack imposter
> after thus depriving him
> of life

This is indeed a rare type of gravestone inscription. I should like very much to know what malady young Mr. Sheffield had and who the "quack imposter" was.

There is perhaps a very interesting bit of history connected with the Sheffields and this farm where the Byrds have lived so long. It appears that Patrick H. Sheffield's father owned it and was living there at the time of the young man's death.

This is perhaps the same farm formerly owned by a Samuel H. Doxey. In The **North Alabamian** for April 12, 1878, is a reproduction of an advertisement that appeared in that paper in 1836 by "Old Joe Sheffield" offering a farm for sale. He described the scenery and the advantages of the place in picturesque style and he said the farm was four miles from Tucumbia, on Bear Creek and was formerly owned by Samuel H. Doxey.

(Continued in next issue of the Quarterly).

COLBERTIANS

By R. L. James

SECTION III CONTINUED

On a high hill a little west of the Barton Road, and about two miles northwest of Crooked Oak in Wheeler Beat, is a very small family cemetery with gravestones bearing the following inscriptions:

JOSIAH FOSTER
BORN
March 5, 1807
DIED
July 24, 1888
His memory is blessed

ELIZABETH M. FOSTER
July 19, 1835
Oct. 5, 1899
She died as she
lived, a Christian

There is nothing unusual about the inscriptions but these graves and one of a daughter, Sallie E. Foster (1856-1901), have the headstones at the east end of the graves instead of the west! It is the usual custom, in this part of the world at least, to bury people with their heads to the west. For some reason, religious, or other, Mr. Foster, so I have heard, requested to be buried with his head to the east. Personally I see no reason why people should have any set rule as to the direction people should be buried. But most of us are such slaves to convention and formality that we dare not offend their dictates.

Josiah Foster came from middle Tennessee before the war and at one time ran a tan yard at Frankfort, so I have been told. His wife was Elizabeth Mary Yarbrough, and as the reader will see from the inscriptions, she was much younger than Mr. Foster. For a great many years they lived on the land on which they were buried, and a better family perhaps did not live in Colbert County. Mr. and Mrs. Foster lived a plain life—far different from that of many of the families in the valley just a few miles away—but they were intelligent, very industrious and economical, and accumulated a good estate. Best of all (according to information from many different persons) they were devout Christians. An old gentleman, a Mr. Kimbrough, who lived with this family for years and who is of no relation to them, told me that **every one** of the family was a good person. Mr. and Mrs. Foster were the parents of two sons, George and Richard, and several daughters. Mrs. S. E. Kimbrough, of Barton, the youngest child is the only one now living. F. Srygley in "Larimore and His Boys" said Reuben Yarbrough's spring was considered the source of Rock Creek. He was perhaps the father of Mrs. Foster.

A few miles northward of Cherokee is Mhoontown church and cemetery. In the early days the Mhoon family was one of the best known of that part of Colbert County. The Mhoons, Prides, Lanes, Rutlands, Bartons, Carlosses, Malones and Goodloes were large landowners and lived in that style of which so much has been written concerning the "Old South."

On a rise in the cemetery we find several very large, elegant monuments containing the names of Mary Mhoon, William S. Mhoon, James E. Mhoon, James George Mhoon, Lucinda W. Mhoon, and Letitia Cotten and with more information recorded than I have seen on any other gravestones. I am here reproducing two inscriptions as follows:

I.

This monument is
erected to the memory
of

MARY MHOON
who was born in
Bertie Co., N. C.
Oct. 5, 1758 &
Died in Tuscumbia
Ala. Oct. 16, 1838
In death and for many
years before she
enjoyed a most perfect
assurance of immortal life
She was the daughter

of Moses Spivey &
Jemima his wife
Moses S. was born
Oct. 19, 1729 & died
Aug. 2, 1771 & was
the son of
Joshua Spivey & Alice
his wife
She was married
to James Bate
June 20, 1776
who died June 3,
1787. Again married
to James Mhoon Feby.
18, 1790 who was born
Nov. 12, 1761 &
died March 4, 1816
Jemima the mother
was born Nov. 4, 1734
and was the daughter
of Jonathan Stanly
& Mary his wife

II.   This monument is
erected to the memory
of

WILLIAM S. MHOON
Born in Bertie Co., N. C.
December 25, 1801
Died in Franklin Co., Ala.
December 26, 1844
Aged 43 years
William Spivey Mhoon
was the son of
John Mhoon and Mary
  his wife
John was born in
Martin Co., N. C. 25th
Novr. 1761 and
Died March 4th, 1816
He was the son of
Josiah Mhoon &

Mourning his wife
Mary Mhoon was
born in Bertie Co.
N. C. Oct. 5, 1758
died in Tuscumbia
Ala. Oct. 16, 1838
She was the daughter of Moses Spivey
and Jemima
his wife

In addition to the interesting Mhoon monuments, we find in this cemetery stones containing the names of Askew, Brown, Collum, Beard, James, Patton and others. I am advised that Reuben Copeland, who was Sheriff of Franklin County in the 1870's, and who was widely known in Both Franklin and Colbert, is buried here; but after a careful search of this cemetery on July 20, 1945, I failed to find any monument containng his name. Mr. Copeland died in 1901 and was quite old. I shall reproduce two more records from this cemetery as follows:

I. ELIZABETH N.

wife of

L. B. ASKEW

BORN

Feb. 26, 1804

DIED

July 12, 1884

Here lies a sinner saved by grace

II. N. W. PATTON

BORN

Jan. 17, 1810

DIED

Oct. 17, 1887

Here lies a sinner saved by grace

END OF SECTION III

WORDS OF PRAISE

"Mr. Lemuel Peters was born in Kean, New Hampshire, in 1772. His nationality was Welsh and his father's family were Quakers. They were, I understood, a people of great stoutness and resolution. I knew Mr. Peters very well. He used to say that his father could lift a weight of a thousand pounds. Lemuel Peters married Sarah Minott, who was born in Dummerston, Vermont, in 1770. In religion she was a Puritan and Presbyterian, and French and Irish in blood and nationality. The families of Mr. Peters and wife were amongst the earliest settlers of New England. She was unusually well educated and intelligent, and very fond of reading. She greatly admired the Spectator and Scott's Novels, which appeared, one after another, about the time our county was settled. In their home were books and papers for their children to read, and this accounts for the fact that every son in the family was well educated and belonged to a profession. Their home was one of hospitality where ministers, of all denominations, especially the Presbyterian, were welcomed. Mr. Peters was an ardent Clay Whig. He came South after his marriage in 1808, and settled at Clarksville, Tennessee, and from that place he removed to Lawrence County in 1820 or 1821, and settled near Leighton where he reared a large family of children. Mrs. Peters died here in 1834, and is buried in the 'Leigh Graveyard.' He removed to Bowie County, Texas; but sold out his possessons there in 1836, and on his way to visit New England died 1837, at the house of Dr. Gideon Williams, on Town Creek and was buried by the side of his deceased wife."

From J. E. Saunders' **Early Settlers of Alabama**, p. 110.

Perhaps it is not too much to say that the Peters family was the most cultured family who lived in the Town creek Triangle before the war. An dthere were many families of considerable culture in that area before the war. Among the sons of Mr. and Mrs. Peters were Charles, who was for many years Judge of the County Court in Morgan County; John, a physician, at one time located at Courtland and later went to Texas; Samuel, a lawyer of LaGrange and Tuscumbia; and Thomas M., a lawyer of Moulton. Thomas M. Peters was a very outstanding man. He was a graduate of the University of Alabama, in the class of 1834, and was a friend and patron of learning the remainder of his life. He was much interested in botany and one of the ferns is named in his honor. He was an especial friend of Dr. Charles Mohr who wrote the Plant Life of Alabama, published in 1901, and in that work s a picture of Dr. Mohr and Judge Peters taken together. Judge ePters was Associate Justice of the Supreme Court of Alabama in 1868 and was Chief Justice in 1873. He was opposed to Secession and leaned to the Union side. Following the war he was very unpopular with many of the people and some very harsh things were printed against him in the papers. However, Colonel Saunders did not use such bitter criticism in his discussion of him in **Early Settlers of Alabama.** Judge Peters' wife was Naomi S. Lutch of Moulton. She and President Jas. K. Polk were first cousins.

"Maj. Kennerly, for a number of years, was the postmaster at LaGrange. After leaving the mountain he lived on the road from LaGrange to Leighton, at what is now known as the Vinson Place. After Dr. Kumpe purchased the Wilson Place, near Leighton, he sold his place to Dr. Drury Vinson and lived with Dr. Kumpe. He and his wife both died at this place. They lived to a good old age and had many warm friends. It is said that the Kennerly residence at LaGrange was built for a Masonic hall and afterwards changed to a residence. This was a brick building."

From A. A. McGreggor's **History of LaGrange College.**

Dr. George E. Kumpe's second wife was a daughter of Maj. James Kennerly and wife. They also were the parents of Misses Kate and Charlotte Kennerly who were well known residents of Moulton, Alabama, for a long while, and there may have been other children.

"Mr. Halsey was one of our oldest and most respected citizens. He came to this section years ago from Virginia. In 1848 he joined the Presbyterian church, lived an exemplary Christian life, and died respected and honored by a large circle of relatives and friends."

From obituary of James Halsey in **Alabama & Times** for January 19, 1871.

According to his gravestone record in Tuscumbia's Oakwood Cemetery, Mr. Halsey was born in North Carolina Aug. 2, 1783, and died Jan. 12, 1871. The descendants of Mr. Halsey have been among the best known and most outstanding people of Tuscumbia.

"Jonathan Barclay was a man of integrity and principle and leaves to those who survive him, the imperishable heritage of an untarnished name.

"He came to Tuscumbia from Fayetteville, Tenn., 1818, and had resided here ever since, highly esteemed by all who knew him.

"We are informed by Mr. Benj. Pybas, one of our oldest and most honored citizens, that the first sermon preached in Tuscumbia was preached in the house of Capt. Barclay."

From obituary of Capt. Jonathan Barclay in the **Alabamian & Times** for June 30, 1870.

Capt. Barclay was a North Carolinian and died June 28, 1870, in the "86th year of his age." His wife died Aug. 8, 1873; their daughter, Mrs. Trotter, died July 3, 1874, and their son, Dr. Anderson Barclay, died July 20, 1875. I do not know just how many children Capt. and Mrs. Barclay had but they had one daughter who married a Mr. McClung. It appears that this was a most respectable and worthy family of people.

From an **Early History of Tuscumbia** by "H" in the **Tuscumbia Democrat** published in installments in 1881-1882 we are advised that the sermon preached in Capt. Barclay's house of which Mr. Pybas spoke was preached by a young Cumberland Presbyterian minister from Lincoln County, Tennessee, named Aaron Alexander. This Mr. Alexander was already known to Capt. Barclay. He later became a leading preacher in his denomination, so states Mr. "H."

A word here about Benj. Pybas. He was a cabinet maker and an undertaker and an amateur geologist of note. Just recently I was shown a beautiful cupboard in one of the Tuscumbia homes made by him. The lady who showed it to me is now in her eighties and was reared a few miles out in the country from Tuscumbia. She said they had the cupboard wrapped to carry home and were very careful not to damage it as they prized it very highly. He is said to have had a fine knowledge of geology and we find on one occasion in 1872 where he read a paper on the geology of Colbert County to a farmer's club. His wife must have taken quite an interest in gardening as she presented one of the local newspaper editors once with an extra large beet grown in her vegetable garden. According to the **North Alabamian** for June 29, 1883, Mr. Pybas was born in Madison County, Alabama, in May, 1808, and died June 29, 1883. The **North Alabamian** said he was probably the oldest native Alabamian in the State at the time of his death and with the exception of "the venerable Mrs. Clay" had lived longer in Tuscumbia than any other citizen. He was a Mason and was buried with Masonic rites. Mrs. Pybas lived until August 6, 1894. She died at Monte Sano, but was buried in Tuscumbia's Oakwood Cemetery where Mr. Pybas was buried. They were the parents of several children. Their daughter, Anna Pybas, was one of the most distinguished teachers in North Alabama, having taught at Tuscumbia, LaGrange and other places.

John Fletcher Pride "Was the son of a Methodist minister who lived to be upward of ninety years old, and was born near Raleigh, N. C., August 26, 1791. He moved to Decatur, Ala., in 1816 and settled at Tuscumbia in 1818, engaging in the business of hotel keeping on the corner now occupied by Whittemore and Hyde. Eight or ten years afterwards he married Miss Susan Barrett of Tuscumbia who was also a North Carolinian and came from the vicinity of Weldon. Her father also lived to be more than ninety years old. He only lived in Tuscumbia a few years before he bought the lands around Pride's Station where he spent three-fourths of a century in the successful pursuit of agriculture and in the practice of every Christian virtue. . . . .

"In the good old days of camp meetings Bishop Paine and many famous divines were regular visitors at his house, and he was never happier than when it was full of preachers. History furnishes few such characters as Mr. Pride's. He was a man of great firmness, and the most rigid and exact integrity, and the clearest and safest judgment, and yet we are told by his son, Dr. J. P. Pride, that he never knew him to lose his temper. Where is there another life so complete, so well rounded? No petulance, nor childishness marred the calm and serene flow of his latter days, and to the last hour, he took a deep interest in his children and his grandchildren as well as in the welfare of his friends and neighbors. As a wise friend, a safe counselor, a devout Christian and a model citizen he will be greatly missed by the community. As the Patriarchal head of a large family he can never be replaced, but instead of tearful words of condolence we beg leave to tender them our sympathetic joy at the beautiful ending of a pure and spotless life, the history of which will ever be their most precious legacy."

From obituary of John Fletcher ("Jack") Pride in the **North Alabamian** (A. H. Keller, Editor) for June 19, 1891.

An article in the **North Alabamian** (A. H. Keller, Editor) for Oct. 31, 1890, has some good things to say of Mr. Pride. Among them was this: "His life has been that of a humble faithful Christian gentleman, whose word is as good as his bond which was always legal tender wherever he was known."

Mr. Pride was a man of large wealth and fine intelligence. He kept up with the news of the times to the end of his life. He was always a strong Democrat. He lived to be almost one hundred years old and passed peacefully away shortly after retiring to bed, on the evening of June 19, 1891, at the home of his son-in-law, Mr. Thompson.

John Fletcher Pride was the son of Maj. Edward Pride whose life is noted in Vol. 6, No. 4 of the Alabama Historical Quarterly—the number which is devoted to the Revolutionary Soldiers buried in Alabama. Maj. Edward Pride is buried in the Pride Cemetery near the place where the "Hock Pride Mountain Road" enters the Lee Highway about four or five miles west of Tuscumbia. According to his gravestone Major Pride was born Nov. 30, 1755, and died Feb. 7, 1839. He had a large family of children who played an important role in the early history of what is now Colbert County. In the cemetery where Maj. Edward Pride is buried may also be found markers containing names of Thomas Pride (May 16, 1808-Oct. 18, 1839, H. J. Pride (1811-May 27, 1889) and Eliza M., wife of H. J. Pride (1824-Mar. 7, 1879). H. J. Pride, known as "Hock" or "Hawk" Pride, was a successful farmer. In one of the Tuscumbia papers for 1872 is notice of an extra fine crop of wheat grown by him. That part of Little Mountain near where he lived is yet referred to as the "Hock" or "Hawk" Pride Mountain.

Another son of Major Edward Pride was Nathaniel Pride, a large planter with a large family. One of his daughters married John Tompkins, and her son, Pride Tompkins, was Probate Judge of Colbert several terms.

The Lane and Carloss families were among others of blood relation to the Prides.

Philip Palmer "was a man of large and varied information and especially well posted in the history of his country. He enjoyed the confidence and esteem of the entire community in which he had lived longer than any who survive him, and leaves the precious legacy of a good name and an honest character to a large family of children, grandchildren and great grandchildren. Of remarkable health and vigor up to within a short time of his death, he suffered but little and passed peacefully away to his rest."

From obituary of Philip Palmer in the **North Alabamian** (A. H. Keller, editor) for July 25, 1879.

Mr. Philip Palmer was born at, or near, Schenectady, N. Y., August 27, 1792, and died July 11, 1879. His wife was Mary Bowers, also from the state of New York. They moved to Limestone County, Alabama, at an early date and not long afterward they removed to Tuscumbia. Among the children of Philip and Mary Palmer was a daughter, Ann E. "who died July 9th, 1841, in the 17th year of her age," and Charles B. who married Isabella Anderson, a native of Rockingham County, Virginia. Miss Anderson came with her father to Tuscumbia "in 1835." Dr. Charles R. Palmer, son of Chas. B. and Isabella (Anderson) Palmer, was a distinguished physician and was perhaps the most distinguished of all the descendants of Philip and Mary Palmer. He married Sudie Huston, a daughter of Dr. James M. and Annie (Barton) Huston.

"Mrs. Felton was the owner of many valuable servants and realized a good income from the hire of them. She also kept boarders, and had washing done for young men in college. She spent much of her money and time in the cultivation of flowers and adorning her home.

"She was an elegant lady. She was educated, practical, refined, modest, yet firm in the discharge of her duty. She was a woman of unswerving faith in God. She never doubted His promises to those who put their trust in Him. In the latter part of her life she was often in stringent circumstances, as her servants were liberated and her income was at an end. Dr. Wadsworth, who had married her daughter in his first marriage, and their friends and relatives furnished her a support. She had many friends who were ready to do for her. She was the sister of ex-Gov. Swain of North Carolina, a sister of Mrs. Blakemore of Shelbyville, Tenn., and aunt of White Blakemore.

From A. A. McGregor's **History of LaGrange College.**

Mrs. Elizabeth Felton to whom Prof. McGregor paid such a nice tribute in his History of LaGrange College was the wife of J. B. Felton. I have no information relating to the life of J. B. Felton except that he was related to Thaddeus Felton who married a daughter of Hartwell King, Sr. She was a resident of LaGrange for many years.

Prof. John C. Stephenson in one of his articles published in the **Leighton News** many years ago tells us that Thomas Bell Wilson, a minister, married Mrs. Martha Ann Felton, "a wealthy widow." She was the mother of Thaddeus Felton, above referred to, and of Hilliard Felton. By Mr. Wilson she had two daughters, Mary Ann and Belle. These two sisters married two Gregg brothers.

Prof. Stephenson writes interestingly of Thomas Bell Wilson. He tells us that he was a graduate of an East Tennessee college and was an author. He was very intelligent, six feet high, weighed one hundred and eighty pounds, carried himself erect, was of fair complexion and could preach two sermons a day (each an hour long) without affecting his voice. He was a Presbyterian and was Pastor of Concord Church in Lawrence County. Prof. Stephenson says he came to North Alabama in 1830 and lived two miles northeast of Leighton. In 1847, according to Prof. Stephenson, the Wilsons moved to Marshall, Texas. Hilliard Felton never married and was a lawyer at Marshall. Thaddeus Felton remained in Alabama, and at one time had charge of the steward's hall at LaGrange College. He and Mrs. Felton were the parents of a prominent family of children.

"This venerable citizen (Andrew Braden) died at his residence southeast of Tuscumbia yesterday evening.... He was a man of the strictest integrity, and by energy and enterprise, had accumulated quite a fortune at the commencement of the war."

From the **North Alabamian** (A. H. Keller, editor) for June 10, 1875.

"Esquire Braden moved to this county in the early settlement of the country. He was one of our oldest citizens. He was an honest and upright man."

From obituary of Andrew Braden in the **North Alabamian** for June 17, 1875.

Mr. Braden was born in Campbell County, Tennessee, July 31, 1797, and died June 9, 1875. He was twice married. His first wife was Jane Pride and his second wife was Martha Pope. All of his children, five sons, were born of the first marriage. Only one of these five sons married. This was William, who married Martha Petree. Miss Petree's parents lived near Barton, and lived at Frankfort in time of the war. One of Andrew Braden's sons died at Camp Douglass and another died near Moulton during the war, both being Confederate soldiers. The names of the four Braden sons who never married were Barton, Jackson, John and Armistead.

"Mr. Horn was a man of strict integrity of character and benevolent disposition. He possessed strong common sense and a well balanced mind. The subject of religion occupied his thoughts for several years before his removal to Texas, and he was troubled with doubt and uncertainty; but more than a year ago he became satisfied of its truth, united with the Episcopal Church, and died in the blessed hope of immortality. Thus has passed away one who will long live in the recollection of the citizens of Tuscumbia, not only for charity and benevolence, but also for the uniformed uprightness of his character.

"A FRIEND."

From obituary of Josiah Horn in the **North Alabamian** for October 20, 1876.

Josiah Horn has already been mentioned as running a steam mill (in connection with Daniel Spangler) on Poplar Creek which Prof. John C. Stephenson said was the first steam mill in North Alabama. Mr. Horn was born in Nash County, North Carolina, in 1798 and died at San Marcos, Texas, Oct. 3, 1876. He came to Alabama in 1817 and lived for many years in Colbert County, moving to Texas about 1872. Prof. Stephenson says Josiah Horn's first wife was a sister of Davis Gurley, a large planter, who lived one mile west of Leighton, and that his second wife was a niece of Mr. Gurley. At one time Mr. Horn kept hotel in what was known as the Central House in Tuscumbia, "was a man of considerable property." He had a daughter, Mollie Horn, who was well educated, talented, and accomplished in music. She was married three times. Her first husband was Capt. W. H. Hunt who was the commandant of cadets at LaGrange College and Military Academy and professor of drawing, and later was a major in the Thirty-Fifth Ala. Reg. After Maj. Hunt's death she married Dr. James Delony and moved with him to Arkansas. Dr. Delony did not live many years; then she went to LaGrange and lived with her father who was then a resident of that classical village. After going to Texas she was married to Mr. Littlepage, a prominent Methodist minister, and lived at Waco. It appears that Mollie Horn was a most worthy character and although she had three husbands in her lifetime, she never went through the disgraceful act of desertion and suing for divorce. She died at her home just outside the city limits of Waco, Texas, June 11, 1912, "aged 72."

Major David Deshler was one of the most prominent citizens Tuscumbia ever had. He was born in Lehigh County, Pennsylvania, Sept. 10, 1798, and died at Tuscumbia Dec. 6, 1871. The writer of his obituary said that he had resided at Tuscumbia more than forty years. Among the things he wrote about Major Deshler was this:

"Major Deshler was no ordinary man; of strong natural abilities, a close penetrating mind, cool clear judgment, and of good education, there was scarcely any subject within the range of human thought or speculation he had not investigated. No one within the writer's knowledge had a more comprehensive store of general information on so great a variety of subjects. He is identified with the early history of the State and was the pioneer in the South of that great system of railways which now add so much to the wealth and prosperity of the entire country. Under his supervision and mainly through his instrumentality the first railroad in Alabama was constructed from Tuscumbia to Decatur.

"Charity with him was a principle, to the needy he was never known to turn a deaf ear, or to refuse his sympathy and aid to the suffering humanity."

All through life Major Deshler was a man of action. Shortly before he died he made a trip to Philadelphia. He had no relatives in Colbert County when he died, at least no close relatives. Mrs. Deshler had died in 1854 and later his oldest son died, suddenly, while a pupil at West Point Academy, and last his son, James, was killed at Chickamauga. Major Deshler gave the grounds and building of the old Deshler Female Institute to Tuscumbia as a memorial to his son, Gen. James Deshler. The Deshler High School at Tuscumbia helps to perpetuate his memory.

"Col. John T. Abernathy certainly deserves a prominent place in the history of LaGrange as no man was more interested in the success of the college and gave more liberally of his time and money and advice.

"He was fully competent to plan for success in any business transaction, and especially could he see the dangers ahead and thwart the intrigues of his opponents. . . . If a man was needed to push forward any interest, he searched for him until found, and used whatever means necessary to secure his services. Being a good judge of men he seldom made a mistake.

"If money was needed he freely gave of his own means, and solicited contributions from others. He was a safe counselor in the discipline of young men, and the rules and regulations, were submitted to his judgment. Successful in his own business he could safely be trusted with any public interest. His home was two miles north of Leighton. He was one of the early settlers, and although he started in life comparatively a poor man, yet by industry and financial skill, he succeeded in accumulating a handsome fortune. He was a member of the Cumberland Presbyterian Church, holding his membership at Mount Pleasant, five miles north of Leighton. He was one of the leading members of his church and contributed liberally to the support of the ministry and other interests. He died soon after the Civil War, having lived to old age."

From McGregor's **History of LaGrange College.**

Col. Abernathy, according to his gravestone record, was born Dec. 8, 1799, and died July 27, 1869. He is buried in a family cemetery near where he lived. Among others buried there, in addition to his two wives, are David Abernathy (1772-Sept. 5, 1845) and Lavenia Abernathy (1776-Mar. 13, 1843). I suppose these were his father and mother. Col. Abernathy's first wife was Sarah Ellett. I believe she was a sister of Deacon Edmund Ellett and John Ellett who lived near Spring Valley. I know she was closely kin to them, if not their sister. His second wife was Eliza Wright. Col. Abernathy was the father of several children. His son, Dr. Robert Townes Abernathy, was a physician of note and a citizen of Tuscumbia. He was a graduate of LaGrange College, and his wife was a daughter of Geo. W. Carroll, a large planter, who lived in the early days near Tuscumbia and later removed to Arkansas. James W. Abernathy, another son, was also a graduate of LaGrange College and was "fond of books." He lived and died at, or near, the old home place. These two sons were born to the first wife of Col. Abernathy.

"Robert McGary Richardson departed this life December the 6th, 1889, aged 89 years, 10 months, and 26 days. He was born in Maury County, Tennessee. He moved to Monroe County, Mississippi, where he married Martha R. Edington in early life and remained there until about the year 1846, and then moved to Franklin County, Ala., when Franklin and Colbert were one. Since they were divided he has resided in Colbert, 4½ miles west of Tuscumbia. He leaves behind 76 descendants, consisting of children, grandchildren and great-grandchildren. He was an old-time and true-blue Democrat. He never, once in his life, voted a mixed ticket. He furnished 6 sons and 3 sons-in-law who fought gallantly for the cause of the South. He believed in churches and religion and was a great Bible reader. He was of a happy and cheerful disposition. Loved company and the society of friends, and had many true and warm ones, wherever he lived."

From obituary of Robert McGary Richardson in the **Southern Idea**, Russellville, Ala., for Jan. 17, 1890.

The writer of Mr. Richardson's obituary failed to state that he was married a second time to Mrs. Louisa Wingo on Dec. 30, 1873, at her home in Colbert County, by John N. Green, and that they lived for sometime in the present Franklin County near Russellville. Mr. Richardson had several children who married into Franklin County families. Two of his daughters married Addison Malone. His son, Henry, married a daughter of Andrew Jackson Willis of the Duncan Creek section, and the youngest son, "Dal," married a daughter of Edwin Vinson, an early settler of Franklin. One daughter married Calvin Enlow who lived for many years in Franklin. He had several other sons who lived and died in Colbert, near Bear Creek Church. From these sons and daughters of Mr. Richardson and his first wife have sprung a host of people. He also had a number of relatives in the early settlement of what is now Colbert, and if all the descendants of these were to assemble together it would be a multitude indeed. His second wife had several children by her former husband, Mr. Wingo, but I do not know anything about her early life nor of her husband's.

"Mrs. Winston was born and married in Virginia and came to this vicinity in its early settlement, where she has lived in affluence, surrounded by loved ones, having raised a family of five daughters and one son.

"She died a Christian, a consistent member of the Episcopal Church. One by one those of the old regime are passing away, until very soon the present generation will have none of them left in our midst to remind us of the memories of 'auld lang syne,' the days of social joys and pleasures in this happy valley, half a century ago."

From obituary of Mrs. Catherine B. Winston in the **North Alabamian** for Aug. 1, 1884.

Mrs. Winston was the wife of Isaac Winston, a large planter who lived near Spring Valley. Her maiden name was Catherine B. Jones, so states one of her great granddaughters, Miss Burt of Tuscumbia. The Isaac Winston home was among the most elegant in the county, being a brick mansion seated on a low hill near the foot of Little Mountain and commanding a lovely view of the valley. It was called "Belle Monte"; and no doubt many gay social functions were held there in the days of "auld lang syne." Isaac Winston was a son of the Revolutionary soldier, Anthony Winston, noted on page 675 of the **Alabama Historical Quarterly**, Vol. 6, No. 4. The Winstons and relatives included such important characters as Gov. John Anthony Winston, Judge John A. Steele, Gov. Robert Burns Lindsay, Maud Lindsay and many others. Isaac Winston died August 13, 1862, aged 68, and Mrs. Catherine B. Winston died July 25, 1884, in "the 84th year of her age."

"He (John G. Shine) was an old and highly esteemed citizen in the 74th year of his age. He walked about on Monday, ate his supper, and rested well till a few minutes before he died. He called someone and by time his family could get to him he died. He settled here some time in December 1825 and became a prominent and successful planter."

From obituary of John G. Shine in **Alabamian & Times** for Sept. 17, 1874.

According to Mr. Shine's gravestone in Tuscumbia's Oakwood Cemetery he was born in Halifax Co., N. C., July 29, 1801, and died Sept. 15, 1874. See sketch of William Cooper family in section II and list of those whose real-estate in 1850 was valued at $5000 and above.

"Dr. Desprez, descended from French and Irish nobility, came to America in 1843, and settled at Buzzard Roost, later went to Cherokee as one of its founders, then moved to Tuscumbia after the war. He was a distinguished scholar, a Christian gentleman of the highest order, a devout Catholic, a Democrat, a Southern sympathizer who gave his sons for the cause, and a physician noted throughout Alabama."

From Leftwich's **Two Hundred Years at Muscle Shoals**, p. 239.

According to his gravestone record in Tuscumbia's Oakwood Cemetery, Dr. Wm. Desprez, of whom Miss Leftwich spoke so highly, was born in Paris, France, in March 1806 and died Oct. 16, 1878. He fell a victim to yellow fever which caused so many deaths in 1878 at various places in the South. He was unselfishly doing his duty when he was overcome by the dread disease. His wife, Susan Deprez, was born in Dundalk, Ireland, Sept. 18, 1808, and died March 16, 1894. They had an interesting and prominent family of children.

"He (Dr. Wm. H. Newsum) was the type of true and noble manhood, his home always the nucleus of a genuine and cultivated hospitality. Small in physical proportions, he possessed the untiring will and energy that carried him so successfully to the zenith of his profession.

"Gentle as a woman in his administrations of duty, his skill and attainments won at once the patient's confidence and esteem. Liberal as a prince, his charities were unheralded and unknown save where his generosity was recognized and felt. How often do I recall sweet memories around his cheerful fireside. Passionately fond of music, and all the refinements of social culture, his home was the radiation of pleasure and happiness. But after life's fitful fever he has gone. Peace to his ashes and a tear to his memory."

Excerpt from a letter by "C" of Huntsville, Alabama, to A. H. Keller, editor of the **North Alabamian**, and dated Apr. 3, 1882.

Mr. "C" states he became a citizen of Tuscumbia nearly 35 years ago. Of Dr. B. F. Newsum he said, "He is a noble specimen of the Creator's handiwork, the 'Abou BenAdhem' of his tribe."

See the Newsums in connection with the Edward H. Newsom family in Section II.

Mr. "C" also lists Drs. Huston, Helms, Mattingly, Barclay and Keller as Tuscumbia physicians "whose scientific attainments would have reflected honor upon any city."

In regard to the lawyers of Tuscumbia in those years before the war Mr. "C" referred to Wm. and Lydal Cooper contrasting these noted brothers, and mentioned Townes, Norman, Armstrong, Cockrill and Nooe, all as being lawyers of high integrity and of ability.

"Mrs. Cannon was born January 1808. She was long and favorably known in this community and commanded the universal esteem of all who knew her. As a wife and mother she was affectionate and attentive as a neighbor, she was proverbial for her kindness and social qualities. To the sick and afflicted she was generous and unceasing in her ministrations. She lived to a ripe old age and leaves many friends and relatives behind who have the pleasing assurance that their loss is her eternal gain."

From obituary of Mrs. Agnes Cannon in **Alabamian & Times** (Jos. Shackelford, Publisher) for Sept. 29, 1870.

Mrs. Agnes Cannon and her husband, John Cannon, are buried in the Oakwood Cemetery at Tuscumbia. Her gravestone states that she was born Jan. 27, 1808, and died Sept. 22, 1870. John Cannon was born May 28, 1800, and died Feb. 3, 1859.

"As a man and a Mason, we shall not soon look upon his like again—faithful and true in his devotion to his friends and country, and zealous in his endeavors to promote the general happiness of man—the Masonic fraternity of this immediate section are indebted to him perhaps more than to any other man living or dead for their prosperity—material and otherwise—and our hearts are sad within us this day with the thought that we shall look upon his face no more."

The above tribute of respect fo rF. G. Norman from Hall of Royal Arch Chapter, Tuscumbia, Ala., is dated Aug. 10, 1885, and is signed by W. R. Julian, J. D. Inman, I. T. Cooper, committee; W. T. Rowland, H. P.

The **Clarion** of Tuscumbia (Blake & Son, Publishers) said Mr. Norman was "one of our best, most respected citizens."

He and his wife are buried in the Oakwood Cemetery at Tuscumbia. He was born in Rutherford County, Tennessee, Jan. 4, 1808, and died Aug. 5, 1885. Felix Grundy Norman was a lawyer of note, represented Franklin County in the Legislature a number of times and was mayor of Tuscumbia for many years.

Mrs. Norman before her marriage was Jane L. Cook, a daughter of Henry and Jane Cook and a sister of Mrs. Amanda Barton. She was born in Huntsville, Ala., Feb. 22, 1824, and died June 25, 1901.

Mr. and Mrs. Norman were the parents of several well known children.

"We were prepared to hear of the death of Mr. J. W. Rutland of Cherokee last Friday as he had been in very feeble health for a long time. He was one of the oldest citizens of this county, and was universally esteemed for his sterling qualities. He was a man of quiet impulses and strong conviction, a kind and hospitable neighbor and useful and influential citizen. He was surrounded by a large family of children and grandchildren, bearing testimony to the last to the truth and comfort of the Christian religion, the profession of which as a member of the Methodist Church he adorned for many years."

From **North Alabamian** (A. H. Keller, editor) for Feb. 1, 1884.

Mr. Rutland was born in Bertie County, North Carolina, Nov. 9, 1808, and died Jan. 25, 1884. He came to the Cherokee community at an early date, and was married to Margaret Barton on Aug. 22, 1833. They had a large family of children. Mrs. Rutland died in 1855 and later Mr. Rutland married her sister, Hannah Maria. The children of John W. Rutland who lived to be grown and married, married into such prominent families as the Scruggs, Goodloe, Pride and Stubbs of Alabama and the Doss of Tennessee and the Ross of Mississippi. Mr. Rutland had one son, John Armistead Rutland, who was killed in the Battle of Shiloh. His sons, James and Wells, were twins.

I mentioned in Section II that the wife of Edward H. Newsom, who lived near Cherokee, was Penelope Rutland. But Mrs. Maude Craig of Jasper, Alabama, who furnished me data on the J. W. Rutland family, says Mrs. Newsom was not related to the I. W. Rutland family. The 1850 Census report also lists as living in Franklin County at that time, Whitman Rutland, aged 68, and possessing real estate valued at $10,000; and Dr. Turner Rutland, aged 64, and Joseph J. Rutland, aged 26. These were perhaps related to Mrs. Newsom.

"Lem Cockburn, as he was familiarly called, has been identified with Tuscumbia since our earliest recollection, and through all the vicissitudes of his family and this community, we have never heard an unkind word spoken of him. He was universally kind and sympathetic and actuated by generous impulses of far beyond his ability to express or perform."

From obituary of G. L. Cockburn in the **North Alabamian** (A. H. Keller, editor) for March 9, 1877.

Mr. Cockburn died of pneumonia on March 9, 1877, in the 66th year of his age. He was a member of the Methodist Church for many years and was tiler of the Masonic lodge. His father was Theophilus W. Cockburn, a very early settler. In the **Early History of Tuscumbia** by "H" we find an account of a very exciting election in 1820, especially the election of Colonel of the 37th Regiment. The two candidates were Theophilus Cockburn and William Parham. The latter was elected; and according to Mr. "H" the reason he was elected was because he had a lot of liquor freely distributed to the voters on the day of the election. The town of Tuscumbia gave Mr. Parham a great majority and much prejudice followed. Mr. "H" said the following about Mr. Cockburn:

"Mr. Cockburn was the father of the late G. L. Cockburn of Tuscumbia, and Mrs. Lavinder of your town. He was a good farmer, an accommodating neighbor, and a highly respected citizen. He died many years ago five or six miles Northeast of Tuscumbia."

Mr. "H" wrote of Mr. Parham as follows:

"Col. Parham was partly raised in Fayetteville, Tennessee, learned the printing business in Huntsville, Alabama, and came to Occoposo among the first settlers. Having married wealthy, he retired from business, devoted his time mostly to politics, was once or twice elected to the Legislature, was second to Henry S. Foote in his duel with Edmund S. Winston in 1827, and died at the residence of Claborne Saunders in Lawrence County in 1828. A man of strong friendship, but also of bitter enmities."

"He was one of our most prominent, enterprising and public spirited merchants, and a man of the most genial, and kindly feelings. He was ever ready to attend the sick or distressed, and it is truly said of him, he was the first at the bed of sickness and last at the grave."

From obituary of John Baxter in **Alabamian & Times** (L. B. Thornton, editor) for Aug. 20, 1874.

Mr. Baxter was a citizen of Tuscumbia for many years. He was a devout Catholic and one of the founders of the Church at Tuscumbia. He served with distinction in the Florida Seminole War under Jackson. He was born in the County of Longford, Ireland, May 10, 1811, and died at Tuscumbia of apoplexy August 14, 1874. His wife, Ann Carroll Baxter, was born in Belfast, Ireland, May 26, 1816, and died May 21, 1869. They were married in Lincoln County, Tennessee, and came to Tuscumbia in 1841. They had at least three sons. One, Thomas Emmet Baxter, went to Arkansas, married a Miss Monroe, and was killed at Laconia in that state by being thrown from a horse. He died June 12, 1871. He was buried there, I believe, but later was re-interred in Oakwood Cemetery at Tuscumbia where his parents are buried. The other two sons were John and Carroll. John went to New York and became a wealthy wholesale merchant and had a spacious summer home at Asbury, N. J. He died in 1901. Carroll was a citizen of Louisville, Ky., but I do not know when he died or what business he followed.

"Mr. Matthews was for many years a prominent and useful citizen of this place, for a long time editor of the **Franklin Democrat** and subsequently sheriff of the county. Prior to the war he moved to the vicinity of Tupelo, Miss., where he resided since. He was stricken with paralysis several years ago and has lingered in a feeble and almost helpless condition ever since. Our boyhood recollection of Alfred Matthews recall him as an earnest, hard working man, of decided and positive temperament, but of the kindest and most generous feelings. He devoted all the energies of his earlier manhood, whilst blest with health and strength, to the support of a large family, and although dying poor, carried to the grave with him the satisfaction that he had nobly discharged this unselfish duty. He was a strong Partisan and a vigorous political writer."

From obituary of A. C. Matthews in the **North Alabamian** (A. H. Keller, editor) for April 18, 1879.

There is no character listed in Colbertians who perhaps is as interesting to me personally as A. C. Matthews and yet I know very little about him other than what Mr. Keller wrote. As I write these words (Aug. 27, 1946) I doubt that there are a dozen persons in Colbert County who scarcely ever heard of him. It is true that he is mentioned in Leftwich's **Two Hundred Years at Muscle Shoals** as being editor of the **Franklin Democrat**, but I do not believe that any special comment is made regarding him. My mother knew his widow and daughter not many years after he died. She had heard about his being sheriff, but I believe she didn't know that he was ever an editor. My mother's parents, or at least her father, must have admired A. C. Matthews greatly, for one of my mother's brothers was named Franklin Matthews, the "Matthews" being in his honor. So the reader can see why I have such a personal interest in Mr. Matthews' history. His daughter died in October 1945 near Russellville. I had meant to see her and ask her about her father's history but I waited too late. It was after her death that I came across the obituary of A. C. Matthews. I have talked with three of her children, but unfortunately they seem to know very little concerning their grandfather's history. One of them told me that he at one time had some kind of job with the Memphis and Charleston Railroad which Mr. Keller failed to mention. Another one said that he was a high ranking Mason which Mr. Keller also failed to note. One of them said that there were twelve children born to Mr. and Mrs. Matthews but all died young, or fairly young, except three. The daughter I have referred to married William Hall who was reared in Franklin County. A. C. Matthews himself died while on a visit to Tuscumbia on April 14, 1879, and was buried in Oakwood Cemetery. I do not know the date of his birth. I think he was a native of some place in Virginia; and my grandfather might have known him there. His wife was a Miss Little, so say his grandchildren. She taught school some after Mr. Matthews died, and she died in 1914, near Walter Valley, Mississippi.

There was a Solomon Matthews from Virginia who settled at Tuscumbia at a very early date. He had a daughter who married Maj. S. W. L. McCleskey, a man prominent in the affairs of both Colbert and Franklin, and their son, Alfred McCleskey, was sheriff of Colbert about forty years ago. Solomon Matthews may have been closely related to Alfred C. Matthews.

"Spangler can wade through gold waist deep, and not a dollar will stick to him," is the statement that Josiah Horn is said to have made about Daniel Spangler when someone mentioned to Mr. Horn that he put a lot of confidence in young Spangler. That was in the days when Horn and Spangler were running the steammill on Poplar Creek. Throughout his long life Daniel Spangler bore a reputation for honesty.

Mr. Spangler lived in his last years south of Leighton near where Harmony Church now is, and in what was then known as the Roscoe community. There he died on Oct. 30, 1845, ."in the 84th year of his age." He was buried at LaGrange. The **Leighton News** (of which F. W. McCormick was editor and Wm. McCormack was associate editor) said the following about Mr. Spangler:

"Mr. Spangler had been confined to his room for two months before his death, and all that loving hands could do for him was cheerfully and willingly done. Now that he has gone the way of all flesh, we can only add that after a quarter of a century's intimate knowledge of him in business relations and otherwise, we never knew a more upright, honest man. He leaves many sons and daughters to mourn the loss of a good father, and a host of friends and acquaintances to testify to his sterling worth as an honest and worthy citizen. May the God of infinite grace watch over, protect and bless the near and dear ones of our departed friend, Daniel Spangler."

Mr. Spangler was married when a young man to a Miss Mullens. He had a large family of children by her. Two of their sons, James H. and D. L. Spangler, were Colbert County officials and prominent in other ways. After his first wife's death he was married in 1880, to George Ann Ayres, and they had two daughters.

"Mr. Guy was probably the oldest citizen in this immediate vicinity. He was a good citizen, a kind and loving father, and was always ready to lend a helping hand to those in distress."

From death notice of Joseph Albert Guy in the **North Alabamian** for June 17, 1898.

Mr. Guy was born July 10, 1814, and died June 15, 1898. He was the youngest of nine children born to Dr. Joseph and Esther (Sharp) Guy who came from Iredell County, North Carolina, in 1822 and settled about three miles west of Tuscumbia. From reading the gravestones in the Guy cemetery, near where Dr. Guy lived, we learn that Dr. Joseph Guy was born Dec. 29, 1767, and died Aug. 1, 1830. His wife was born April 22, 1770, and died March 22, 1850. Dr. Guy was a graduate of the Philadelphia Medical College and his granddaughter, Mattie Guy of Tuscumbia, now in her 85th year, has his diploma. The nine children of Dr. and Mrs. Guy consisted of six sons and three daughters. It was their son, Lorenzo Guy, from whom the beautiful carriage made by Isaac E. Young, was taken by an unprincipled Federal officer in time of the war. Another son, Martin Guy, was once sheriff. One of their daughters, Esther J., married B. J. Smith and was the mother of the first wife of Dr. W. C. Wheeler of Cherokee, whose obituary I have included in the section on obituaries and cemetery records.

Joseph Albert Guy himself married a daughter of Littleberry and Mary (Battle) Cheatham. Mr. Cheatham was a native of Northampton County, North Carolina. Miss Battle was his second wife and Mrs. Guy was the only child of that marriage. Littleberry Cheatham owned a plantation on Bear Creek southwest of Tuscumbia in the ante-bellum days. There were also other Cheathams in that section who were probably relatives of his.

Joseph Albert Guy and wife had a family of several children. One son, I. P. Guy, has been noticed in connection with the Edward H. Newsom family. His sister, Miss Mattie Guy, tells me that I. P. Guy was first married to a Miss Sewell of Trinity, Ala., which I did not know when I made mention of him.

In the **North Alabamian** for Feb. 8, 1894, comment is made about Joseph Albert Guy having lived for 72 years on the same farm. It said he was 80 years old, in the full enjoyment of health, got around vigorously, and was in Tuscumbia nearly every day. A very interesting record, indeed, which reminds me that James W. Alexander of the Brick community, north of Leighton, is said to have lived 60 years continuously at the same place. According to his gravestone, Mr. Alexander was born Dec. 31, 1821, and died Nov. 8, 1903. It was said that he was an elder in the Mt. Pleasant Cumberland Presbyterian Church, a church member more than 60 years, and the father of 15 children. There were other Alexander families at Brick and as a whole they were substantial folks.

"He (Col. L. B. Thornton) was identified with Tuscumbia for more than fifty years. He represented Franklin County in the Legislature, was for many years an elder in Presbyterian Church, and Register in Chancery, was a high Mason and Knight Templar and served as mayor of Tuscumbia. He was a scholar and man of large reading and in his former years the dispenser of a most generous and liberal hospitality."

From death notice or obituary of Col. Lewis Bedford Thornton in the **North Alabamian** for Jan. 11, 1895.

Col. Thornton was born in Spotsylvania Co., Va., May 28, 1815, and died Jan. 10, 1895. He had suffered from paralysis many weeks before his death. He was twice married. His first wife was Virginia Nooe, a sister of John A. Nooe, "the first graduate of the University of Alabama," and his second wife was Louisa Meredith of Tuscumbia, a daughter of an estimable widow who was one of the distinguished Hogun (or Hogan) family of Colbert.

Col. Thornton made interesting notes about the war, especially about the Federal occupation of Tuscumbia, some of which are included in **Two Hundred Years at Muscle Shoals**. I find that in the summer of 1872 he visited his old Virginia home.

"He (Dr. Wm. Cordwell Cross) had resided in this county thirty or forty years, and leaves a large circle of acquaintances and no enemies who deplore his death and sympathize with his splendid family. He was a splendid physician, a true and honest man, a sincere friend, and a valuable and worthy citizen. He was a surgeon of the 16th Ala. Reg. during the war and greatly beloved by every member of it."

From the **North Alabamian** (A. H. Keller, editor) for Sept. 1, 1882.

The Keller account says he died Aug. 28, 1882, of cancer. On pages 174 and 175 of **Early Settlers of Alabama** by J. E. Saunders is the following statement: "Wm. C. Cross, of Cherokee, Colbert County, was appointed surgeon of the Sixteenth in October, 1861, and was promoted to senior surgeon of the brigade in the spring of 1862 while at Corinth. He remained with the wounded at Perryville, was transferred to hospital duty in the spring of 1863, and remained on duty at Newnan, Ga., until near the close of the war. A brother surgeon who knew him in service intimately says, 'He is a fine physician, a devoted friend, a true patriot, and an elegant gentleman.' He lives at Cherokee.'"

According to records possessed by Mrs. W. D. Brotherton of Cherokee, a granddaughter of Dr. Cross, he was a son of Jesse and Mary (Lawrence) Cross and was born in what is now Gates County, North Carolina, March 20, 1815, and died near Cherokee, August 29, 1882. He was married in Lawrence County, Alabama, on October 20, 1841, to Mary Ann Frances Harris. They were the parents of eight children—three sons and five daughters. One daughter died, a young lady, unmarried; another daughter, Amanda Rebecca, married Thomas Lile from Courtland, Alabama, and the others died in infancy or when small. Two of the sons lived to adult life and married. They were: Benjamin Jesse married Mary Alexander of the Cherokee neighborhood, and William Cyprian (who was also a physician) married (1) Arabella Prince of Tuscaloosa and (2) Lyda Jennings of Newbern, Alabama.

Dr. Cross is said to have been as fond of his pipe as were the Dutch settlers of New Amsterdam or as was "Old King Cole" of the nursery rhyme. It was thought by some, that his almost constant pipe-smoking caused the cancer which killed him. Of course I do not know. While I have never smoked or used tobacco in any form, I believed it is said that pipe-smokers, as a rule, are good-natured folks and from the accounts of Dr. Cross he must have been good-natured—a man of lovable disposition.

"No man has ever lived in the country who did more for the public in advice, actual labor, and contributions of money than Dr. G. E. Kumpe. The Masonic Lodge at Leighton was presided over by him for a number of years, and the lodge under his supervision was classed among the best in the state. His lectures were superior to any I ever heard in any lodge. He was an active steward in the Methodist church and contributed liberally to the support of the ministry. The cause of education had in him a warm advocate and a cheerful and strong supporter. To him we are largely indebted for the success of LaGrange College. He was an especial friend of Bishop Paine and Prof. Tutwiler while they were connected with the college. He also had the high esteem of Dr. Wadsworth and Prof. Hardy who succeeded Bishop Paine and Prof. Tutwiler.

"It mattered not how extended his practice, he would attend his patients, then meet the board of trustees in their deliberations for the interest of LaGrange College. He was a man of superior judgment in business and was often consulted by the best financiers of the country in reference to extensive business transactions."

From **History of LaGrange College** by A. A. McGregor.

Prof. John C. Stephenson writing in the **Leighton News** many years ago said: "Dr. Kumpe was an extraordinary man. He was physically, morally and mentally a perfect man. He was 5 feet, 11 inches high, erect in body, broad-shouldered and symmetrically built, weighed 170 pounds. His voice was full and strong; in his Masonic lectures his accent was clear, though the German brogue clung to him till death. He was distinct in his enunciation. He was a blonde, had a beautiful fair complexion, rosy cheeks, dark nut-brown hair, head large and round, high square forehead, eyes a bright clear blue, face rather oval with regular features, nose thin and regularly curved, mouth small and expressive, perpendicular front teeth, and full round chin.

"Dr. Kumpe was active in the practice of medicine till his last sickness. Indeed, his death was caused by a hurt he received accidentally in attending a patient. He was known in North Alabama as one of the most learned and successful physicians in the profession."

According to Dr. Kumpe's tombstone in the cemetery at LaGrange, he was born Oct. 7, 1819, and died Aug. 29, 1887. He was a native of Germany. He had a brother, John Kumpe, who also came to America and lived in what is now Colbert County. He removed from Colbert to Arkansas, so says Rebecca Kumpe of Leighton. Dr. George E. Kumpe lived in LaGrange when it was a flourishing village and a center of culture. He was married two times and perhaps three. There is a grave in the Oakwood Cemetery at Tuscumbia whose marker states that the person buried there was "Catherine F., consort of George E. Kumpe, departed this life 16th April 1844, aged 21 years and 6 months." The wife with whom he lived so long, and the mother of his children, was Rebecca F. Kennerly (Oct. 1, 1819-Aug. 30, 1874), the daughter of Major and Mrs. Jas. Kennerly. After her death Dr. Kumpe was married to the widow of Dr. Anderson Barclay. Dr. Kumpe was the father of several sons and one daughter who died in childhood. One or two of his sons made doctors and located in Montana. Another one was Probate Judge of Lawrence County for many years. In fact, I believe all of them were quite successful in life.

"We were pained to learn on our return home, of the death of Mr. H. P. Carloss, long a resident of the vicinity of Barton, in this county. He was a North Carolinian by birth, a man of ardent and generous impulses, a thrifty and energetic farmer, a strong friend and a useful citizen."

From the **North Alabamian** (A. H. Keller, editor) for Dec. 2, 1875.

"That few men acted their part better in life than the deceased, is the verdict of a grief stricken community, which now deplores his loss. It is no excess of praise to say of him, he was honest, generous, manly, and brave from boyhood, and the last year of his life was crowned with a devout and happy experience of grace. A man of firm and decided convictions about everything, he was especially so in the matter of religion. Before he assumed the name of Christian, he often assured his Pastor, that he had no recollection that he had ever entertained a doubt, even for a moment, about the authenticity and genuineness of the Christian system or Scriptures. And so when he embraced religion it was from the highest conviction of its necessity to him, and of its paramount claims upon him."

From obituary of H. P. Carloss by W. H. A. (W. H. Armstrong?) in the **North Alabamian** for Dec. 16, 1875, and dated from Cherokee, Ala., Dec. 13, 1875.

Halcott Pride Carloss was born in Chatham County, North Carolina, April 15, 1820, and died Nov. 29, 1875. He was a son of Archelaus and Ruth (Pride) Carloss. His mother was, if I understand correctly, a daughter of Maj. Edward Pride and a sister of John Fletcher Pride who have already been noticed. Mr. Carloss married Laura Patterson of Decatur, Alabama, and to them were born eight children. Only two are now living. They are James A. Carloss of R. F. D. 2, Elkmont, Alabama, and a daughter, Mary, of San Antonio, Texas. James A. Carloss gave me this information in a letter written Aug. 1, 1946, and he says he is 88 years of age.

Mr. Keller in speaking of the death of H. P. Carloss said that he was a "thrifty and energetic farmer." There is a notice in the Alabamian and Times for Jan. 8, 1874, which I here reproduce.

"Large Hogs

"Mr. H. P. Carloss, who lives near Barton, in this county, killed a few days ago, so we are informed, two very large hogs. One weighed 502 pounds and the other 509 pounds. Who can beat this in Alabama?"

A later notice stated that he killed fifteen hogs and that the average weight of the fifteen was considerably over three hundred pounds. The fifteen of course included, I suppose, the extra two large ones. I have made note of this to show that Mr. Carloss knew how to grow large hogs and that there were large hogs in Alabama seventy-two years ago.

H. P. Carloss had a borther, W. J. Carloss, who lived in Colbert County many years and was a highly esteemed gentleman. His obituary in the **Tuscumbia Dispatch** for Aug. 20, 1903 states that he died at the home of his daughter, Mrs. M. A. Hopkins of Sheffield, Ala., Aug. 11, 1903. He was born in North Carolina and his wife was Lucy Grandbury who died Feb. 26, 1896. They were the parents of several children, in addition to Mrs. Hopkins, one being the wife of Dr. Frank T. Gilmore of Colbert County.

There may have been other Carlosses in Colbert that I have no data on. I had forgotten to state that the wife of Halcott Pride Carloss lived until 1920. And in giving the maiden name of Mrs. W. J. Carloss I have used the spelling as used in her obituary. It probably should have been Lucy "Granberry" or "Grandberry."

"Our acquaintance with Capt. Stickles began previous to the war when he was engaged in steam-boating on the Tennessee River, and it affords us pleasure to hear testimony to his high character as a citizen and business man, and to his indomitable courage and devotion as a soldier. He was a Northern man, we think a Pennsylvanian, and yet the South had no more ardent friend nor a more gallant defender."

From obituary of Capt. J. H. Stickles in the **North Alabamian** (A. H. Keller, editor) for April 13, 1883.

According to his gravestone in the Atkisson Cemetery near the site of old Mountain Mills, Capt. Stickles was born April

19, 1827 and died April 5, 1883. It shows also that he was a Mason. The spelling there is "Stickle" and not "Stickles." Mrs. Donley of Tuscumbia, a granddaughter of Hector and Sallie (Franklin) Atkisson, says that Capt. Stickle came from Pennsylvania which confirms Mr. Keller's belief. She says that Capt. Stickle was twice married. She does not know who his first wife was, but his second wife was Elizabeth Old. Miss Old's mother was a sister of Sallie Franklin who married Hector Atkisson. According to her gravestone Elizabeth Old Stickle was born Feb. 10, 1844 and died Jan. 7, 1883—just about three months before Capt. Stickle died.

Capt. Stickle was at one time connected with the Mountain Mills Factory. This factory was two miles south of Barton, at the foot of the mountain, and on the road that connects Barton with old Frankfort, the latter place being at one time the county seat of Franklin County, when the county included what is now Colbert exclusive of the Town Creek-Triangle. W. B. Kimbrough tells me that at one time there was a foundry at Mountain Mills, but the place was best known for the manufacture of thread. I am advised that the Cherry Cotton Mill of Florence, Alabama, is a successor to Mountain Mills Factory.

J. M. DEAN

"We were grieved to learn of the death last week in Cherokee of Capt. J. W. Dean, a gentleman whom it was good to have known. He had been in declining health for a number of years, and though his death was expected, it was nevertheless a sad blow to the family, and the community in which he resided. He was an honest, upright and esteemed citizen respected by a wide acquaintance, and his death will be deeply deplored by his numerous friends. May his soul find rest in the land far beyond."

From **Tuscumbia Weekly-Dispatch** for Nov. 13, 1888.

According to Capt. Dean's gravestone in the cemetery at Cherokee he was born April 13, 1836 and died November 5, 1888. W. C. Holesapple advises me that Capt. Joseph W. Dean married a sister of Dr. W. C. Wheeler, but unfortunately there was a separation. Capt. Dean was one of Cherokee's leading merchants and business men.

"There were but few such men as Sam Aldridge—he was generous to a fault; possessing the **noblest impulses**, with a feeling of the most lady-like purity I ever knew; and I knew him well. He was a gentleman at home and abroad.

"He was always happy and gay and strove to make all pleasant with whom he associated. Everybody liked Sam. He had not an enemy in the world. Altho he was universally liked, he had but few friends in whom he confided.

"He was truly a noble representation of better days and purer times."

From obituary of Samuel H. Aldridge in the **North Alabamian** (by "A Friend") for Jan. 28, 1881. The obituary is dated for Jan. 24, 1881 and according to it Mr. Aldridge was born Oct. 11, 1839 and died June 1, 1880. His wife was Emma L. Barton. Miss Barton's parents were Armistead and Amanda (Cook) Barton. Mrs. Emma Scruggs of Tuscumbia tells me that Samuel H. Aldridge's father was a Philadelphia wholesale merchant, and that Barton Dickson, who had a store at Dickson Station, west of Cherokee, used to go to Philadelphia, and buy goods from Mr. Aldridge. As a result of these contacts with the Aldridges, Samuel H. came to Alabama and married Miss Barton. Mrs. Scruggs has a large painting of this Miss Barton and it shows her to have been a beautiful woman. She also has one of Samuel H. Aldridge. There is a remarkable resemblance in this painting and the pictures of Edgar Allen Poe. These two paintings were the works of a Mr. Frye to whom I have already referred.

THE BARTONS

It appears that Armistead and Amanda Cook Barton were the wealthiest people who lived in Franklin County in their day. The 1850 Census report shows Mrs. Barton's real-estate value to have been $127,000. When I wrote the first two sections of Colbertians, I was seriously in doubt of this. I thought perhaps the Census enumerator made a mistake in his writing and that it was $27,000 instead of $127,000. Even $27,000 was far above the average. But lately I have learned from good authority that the Bartons were very large land and slave owners and also that Armistead Barton was a large stockholder in the Tuscumbia - Decatur Railroad. Mr. Barton died comparatively a young man. He was born in Virginia in 1800 and died in 1847. According to an old Huntsville newspaper, Mr. Barton was married to Amanda Cook on January 20, 1829. She was a daughter of Henry Cook who was born in Rockingham Co., Va., May 21, 1782 and died at Tuscumbia, April 29, 1850. Mr. Cook was one of the pioneers of Huntsville, Ala., but his last years were spent at Tuscumbia, where both he and Mrs. Cook are buried. Amanda Cook, Armistead Barton's wife, was born in 1809 and died in 1884. She therefore lived a widow about thirty-five years.

ARMISTEAD BARTON

AMANDA COOK BARTON

The parents of Armistead Barton were Dr. Hugh and Mary (Shirley) Barton. They were originally from Virginia, later lived in East Tennessee and finally removed to what is now Colbert County, Alabama. The 1850 Census report gives Dr. Hugh Barton's age as 76 and his wife's as 70. They were the parents of twelve children, Armistead being the oldest. Among the other eleven were Arthur and James Shirley Barton, well known citizens of Colbert. I am advised that Barton, Ala., was named for Arthur Barton. He lived to be fairly old and was never married. James Shirley, who was the youngest of the Barton family, married (1) Lizzie Petty, (2) a Miss Hawkins. Hugh, another son of Dr. Hugh and Mary (Shirley) Barton, married Jane Harris and lived at Bastrop, Texas. Among the daughters of Dr. Hugh and Mary (Shirley) Barton were: Elizabeth married Wm. Dickson, Margaret Ann and Hannah Maria, both of whom were married to J. W. Rutland, and Louise Vance married Horace Warren and died in Austin, Texas.

Clark T. Barton was one of the leading merchants of Tuscumbia in the early days. He was a nephew of Dr. Hugh Barton. He was born July 8, 1799 and died Feb. 8, 1848. His wife was Jane B. Aldridge, a granddaughter of Armistead and Amanda (Cook) Barton, and she was born Sept. 10, 1811 and died Jan. 26, 1885. She came to Tuscumbia with her father, Thomas Aldridge (died Dec. 25, 1852, aged 55), from the vicinity of Lynchburg, Virginia. Mrs. Scruggs says that Clark T. Barton's wife was of no relation to Samuel H. Aldridge. It appears that Clark T. and Jane B. (Aldridge) Barton were the parents of several children but that only two lived to adult life. These were Kate who married Col. W. A. Johnson and Clark T., Jr. (called "Veto") who married a Miss Price.

In conclusion of these remarks on the Barton family I should state that Armistead Barton was also a merchant of Tuscumbia in the early days and he and his family lived in the brick house now the home of Mrs. Lula Merril Simpson. He then removed to the vicinity of Dickson Station west of Cherokee.

MISS VIRGINIA WILLIAMS

Miss Virginia Williams deserves special mention for having kept an interesting diary in the days of the war. I have seen this diary. It was written in a beautiful hand but time has faded much of it so badly that it is hard to read. She was a daughter of Prof. Wm. G. and Susan Adelaide (Miller) Williams, the former who was from Massachusetts and who was a professor in LaGrange College and also a Presbyterian minister. Prof. Williams' sympathy was with the Union, but his son became a soldier of the Confederacy much against his father's will. In 1863 Prof. Williams returned to New England, his wife having died in 1859.

Miss Virginia Williams married a Mr. Hobgood. Her son, John Hobgood, who lives a few miles east of Tuscumbia, has a framed record of her death and it reads as follows:

"In Loving Remembrance of

My Dear Wife

Mrs. Virginia M. Hopgood

Died Apr. 13, 1891

Aged 52 years, 4 mo., 25 days"

The name Hobgood was misspelled in this record which I find to be rather a frequent occurrence in tombstone records and other records.

The Hobgoods were among the prominent early settlers in the valley between Tuscumbia and Leighton. I do not have very much information about them, but the gravestone record of

John Hobgood, one of these early Hobgoods, shows that he was born in Halifax County, N. C., Oct. 10, 1800, emigrated to Alabama in 1818, and died Feb. 13, 1859. He married Martha A. Alsobrook, a daughter of Col. William and Alice (,Sessum) Alsobrook. Elijah Hobgood was a brother of John Hobgood.

END OF SECTION IV.

In addition to those mentioned in the preface to Colbertians, I wish to express my appreciation to the following for help in compiling this section:

Miss Mattie Guy, Mrs. Emma Scruggs and Mr. Wm. Borden of Tuscumbia; Mr. James Carloss of Elkmont; Mrs. J. F. Craig of Jasper; Mrs. W. A. Malone and Mrs. W. D. Brotherton of Cherokee; Mr. Ernest Hall and his sisters, Mrs. Crawford and Mrs. Laster of Russellville; and there may be a few others that I have overlooked.

ERRATA AND ADDITIONS 599

p. 175, par. 3, line 1: Hartwell King, Sr. did not have a middle name according to Bible and court records. His son was named Hartwell Richard King, Jr.

p. 184, par. 3, line 3: Dr. Richard G. Croom is buried in the Madding Family Cemetery. He died in Lawrence So., AL, on 1 Dec 1841.

p. 184, par. 3, lines 9-10: Dr. Croom had relatives who came to Lawrence, Franklin, and Green (later Hale) Co., AL, but none were brothers.

p. 188, par. 5, line 2: Miss Jones' given name was Edith. (Lawrence Co., AL, Estate Settlements, Jan 1831.)

p. 188, par. 5, line 4: George H. Hinton should be George W. Hinton. (Bible record and Lawrence Co., AL, Estate Settlements, Jan 1831.)

p. 202, par. 2, line 10: Mrs. Atkisson's maiden name was Sarah W. B. Franklin. She was a daughter of Joel Franklin who died in Amherst Co., VA, in 1807. (Franklin Family Bible record.)

p. 206, par. 2, line 1: William Cooper was a friend and advisor to the Indians in the western part of Franklin Co. He was not a chief.

p. 222, par. 2: The sketch of Franklin County families was published privately as Distinguished Men, Women and Families of Franklin County. It was never published in the Quarterly.

p. 383, par. 2, line 2: Change "years of ago" to "years of age".

p. 388, par. 5, line 2 and p. 389, par. 1, line 1: Nancy E. White died in 1822, not 1882. She was Nancy E. Banton, first wife of Robert Marley White. (White Family Bible record.)

p. 389, par. 1, line 4: Change "obpect" to "object".

p. 396, par. 3, line 3: The head of the Prewit (Preuit) family was William Prewit who was no more than 88 years old at the time of his death. His will, made in Madison Co., AL, in 1812, was proved in 1817. In it, he makes no mention of a wife; she must have preceded him in death. His last child was born ca 1761; possibly his wife died soon thereafter.

p. 508, par. 5, lines 1, 7, and 10: There is no proof that Edward Pride ever held the rank of Major. This rank does not appear on the gravestone nor on his pay vouchers.

p. 510, par. 3, lines 9 and 10: Mrs. Felton, the widow of J. Boon Felton, was a sister-in-law of ex-Gov. Swain, not a sister. Neither was she a sister of Mrs. Blakemore; rather, she was a sister of Mrs. Daniel L. Battinger who was the mother-in-law of Dr. J. A. Blakemore. (Wheeler, J. H. Reminiscences and Memorials of North Carolina and Eminent North Carolinians, 1884-1966; p. 106.)

p. 510, par. 5, line 4: Thaddeus Felton was the son of William Felton who died in Lawrence Co., AL, in 1825. (Lawrence Co., AL, Orphans Court, Feb 1826, p. 46.)

p. 511, par. 1, line 6: 1830 is not correct. Thomas Bell Wilson was in Lawrence Co., AL, as early as 1825. He married Mrs. Martha Ann Eliza Felton, widow of William Felton, on 29 April 1829. (Lawrence Co., AL, Marriage Book B; Lawrence Co., AL, Orphans Court, Nov Term 1829.)

p. 511, par. 1, line 6: 1847 is not correct. Thomas B. Wilson and wife, Martha Ann Eliza Wilson, sold land to John J. Abernathy on 14 March 1849. (Lawrence Co., AL, Deeds, Journal M, p. 289.)

INDEX TO PLACES 601

Aberdeen, MS . . . 187
 190, 394
Alabama 161
 164, 165, 169, 181, 182
 187, 188, 202, 205, 207
 209, 213, 219, 371, 374
 375, 376, 377, 380, 381
 382, 383, 384, 385, 387
 388, 389, 391, 392, 394
 396, 398, 502, 505, 507
 509, 511, 512, 515, 517
 519, 520, 525, 527, 528
 529, 530, 531, 534, 536
Allsboro 212
Alsoboro 164
Amelia Co., VA . . . 202
Amherst Co., VA . . . 391
Anne Arundel Co., MD 384
Arkansas 200
 219, 371, 372, 388, 512
 514, 521, 528
Asbury, NJ 522
Athens 398
Atlanta, GA 185
Austin, TX 534

Bainbridge 168
Baltimore, MD 394
Barton . . 162, 168, 183
 202, 203, 208, 386, 501
 511, 529, 530, 531, 534
Bastrop, TX 534
Bavaria 172
Bear Creek 166, 400, 525
Bear Creek Church . . 182
 515
Bedford Co., TN . . . 390
Bedford Co., VA . . . 391
Belfast, Ireland . . 521
Belgreen 202
Belle Monte 516
Bertie Co., NC . . . 501
 502, 503, 519
Bethel 372
Bethlehem 183
Bibb's Lane 374
Big Bear Creek . . . 164
 165, 166
Billy Sanderson Cave 168
Billy Sanderson Cove 168
Birmingham 374
Blockton 388
Bossier Parish, LA . 194
Bowie Co., TX 504
Boxwood 188
Breslau, Russia . . . 172
Brick . . . 183, 398, 525
Brooklyn, NY 182
Brunswick Co., VA . . 203
Bull-Skull Creek . . 166
Buzzard Roost 163
 385, 517
Buzzard Roost Creek . 165

California 188, 213, 218
Camp Douglas, IL . . 511
Campbell Co., TN . . 511
Cane Creek . . 161, 166

Caney Creek 161
Cape Horn 188
Carolina Co., VA . . 379
Carolinas . . . 162, 169
Charles City Co., VA 375
Chatham Co., NC . . . 529
Cherokee 161
 164, 183, 208, 212, 213
 215, 369, 377, 378, 380
 381, 382, 386, 388, 501
 517, 519, 520, 524, 526
 527, 529, 531, 532, 534
Cherry Cotton Mill . 531
Chickamauga 513
Chickasaw Territory . 166
Cincinnati, OH . . . 220
Clarksville, TN . . . 504
Clinch River 396
Coahoma Co., MS . . . 200
Coal Hill, AR . 161, 219
Coburn Mountain . . . 221
Colbert Co., MS . . . 161
Colbert Heights . . . 168
Cole Co., MO 398
Columbia, TN 394
Columbus, MS 190
Concord Church . . . 511
Connecticutt . 171, 182
Cook's Bluff . 166, 201
Cook's Creek . 166, 197
Corinth, MS . . 185, 526
Cotton Garden 194
County Line Road . . 162
Courtland 168
 194, 389, 504, 527
Crooked Oak 500

David Lipscomb College
 218
Davidson Co., TN 203, 209
Decatur 187
 199, 391, 507, 513, 529
Deshler Female Istitute
 391, 513
Deshler High School . 391
Deshler Institute . . 207
Dickson 384, 385
Dickson Station 532, 534
Donegal, Ireland . . 392
Driskell's Chapel . . 387
Dummerston, VT . . . 504
Duncan Creek 515
Duncan Creek Church . 181
Duncan, MS 161
Dundalk, Ireland . . 517

East Tennessee 510, 534
Edgefield Co., SC . . 206
Edinburgh, Scotland . 391
Elkmont 369, 529
England 165
 172, 216, 389
Ensley 208
Eufala 194
Europe 220

Fairfield, TX 187
Fayette Co., AL . . . 181

Fayette Co., TX . . . 192
Fayetteville, TN 506, 521
First Methodist Church,
 Tuscumbia 201
First Presbyterian Church
 Tuscumbia 206
Flatwoods 197
Florence 161, 212
 218, 370, 382, 383, 531
Fluvania Co., VA 209, 392
Fort DuQuesne 164
Fox-trap Creek 166, 183
France 172
Frankfort . 168, 208, 211
 219, 221, 500, 511, 531
Franklin Co., AL . . 159
 161, 162, 165, 166, 169
 181, 183, 197, 198, 199
 201, 202, 205, 206, 210
 211, 212, 214, 215, 219
 221, 222, 372, 379, 502
 503, 515, 519, 520, 523
 525, 531, 533
Franklin Springs . . 214
Freed-Hardeman College
 219
Fuque's Sawmill . . . 388

Gates Co., NC 526
Geise's Mill 385
Georgetown 164
Georgia 169
 171, 183, 392, 526
Germany 172, 528
Gonzales, TX 190
Good Springs 214
Granville, NC 379
Green Springs Academy 187
Greenwood, MS 203

Hale Co., AL 184
Halifax Co., NC . . . 192
 195, 516, 536
Hanover Co., VA 169, 374
Harrisonburg, VA . . 385
Harmony Church . . . 523
Hawk Pride Mountain . 509
Helena, AR 371
Henderson, TN 219
Hewson Creek 166
Hindman's Mill . . . 385
Hock Pride Mountain . 509
Hock Pride Mountain Road
 508
Horn's Mill 167
Hunter 184, 392
Huntingdon, England . 207
Huntsville . . 161, 220
 378, 517, 519, 521, 533

Indian Territory . . 164
Iredell Co., NC . . . 524
Ireland 168
 172, 373, 392, 517, 521
Iuka, MS . 213, 373, 388
Ivy Point, The . . . 166

Jackson Mill Creek . 166

INDEX TO PLACES

Jackson, MS . . 161, 194
Jackson, TN 192
James Creek 166
Jasper . . 161, 369, 520
Johnson Co., AR . . . 219
Johnston Co., NC . . 191
Jonesboro 221

Kean, NH 504
Kentucky . . . 169, 171
  214, 380, 385, 398, 522

Laconia, AR 521
LaGrange 167
  168, 182, 187, 188, 189
  190, 191, 193, 194, 200
  392, 393, 394, 395, 504
  505, 507, 510, 512, 528
LaGrange College . . . 167
  185, 187, 188, 189, 190
  191, 193, 393, 394, 395
  398, 510, 511, 512, 514
  527, 535
LaGrange Mountain . . 191
LaGrange Road 166
Lake Wilson 168
Lancaster Co., PA . . 384
Lauderdale Co., AL . 161
  165, 382, 387
Lawrence Co., AL . . 161
  162, 164, 167, 168, 181
  185, 188, 190, 194, 197
  216, 371, 372, 391, 395
  504, 511, 521, 526, 528
Lee Highway 508
LeFlore Co., MS . . . 203
Lehigh Co., PA 390, 513
Leighton . 160, 162, 167
  168, 182, 183, 184, 185
  190, 191, 194, 196, 369
  371, 373, 382, 395, 398
  504, 505, 511, 512, 514
  523, 525, 527, 528, 535
Ligon 166, 197
Ligon Springs 166
  182, 197, 198, 200, 201
Limestone Co., AL . . 176
  196, 374, 509
Lincoln Co., GA . . . 392
Lincoln Co., TN 506, 521
Litchfield Co., CT . 182
  206
Little Mountain . . . 221
  509, 516
Littleville . . 168, 197
London, England . . . 392
Longford, Ireland . . 521
Louisiana 192, 220, 383
Louisville, KY . . . 522
Lynchburg, VA 534

Madison Co., AL . . . 203
  214, 396, 398, 507
Maine 171
Manchester, VA . . . 393
Marengo Co., AL . . . 203
Marion Co., AL 165, 214
Mars Hill College . . 218

Mars Hill College . . 219
Marshall, TX 511
Martin Co., NC . . . 502
Maryland . 376, 382, 384
Mason-Dixon Line . . 171
Massachusetts . 171, 535
Maury Co., TN 197
  199, 515
McAfee Creek 166
Mecklenburg Co., NC . 221
Memphis, TN 205
  207, 380, 383
Meridian, MS 161
Mhoontown Church . . 501
Mill Creek 166
Mississippi 161
  164, 176, 194, 200, 203
  211, 212, 384, 388, 394
  515, 520, 522, 523
Missouri . . . 210, 398
Montana 398, 528
Monte Sano 507
Monterey, Mexico . . 213
Montgomery 215
Monroe Co., MS . . . 515
Morgan Co., AL . . . 504
Mose Branch 166
Moulton . . . 213, 216
  377, 395, 504, 505, 511
Mount Holly, NJ . . . 182
Mount Hope 395
Mount Moriah 184
Mount Moriah Church . 202
Mount Pleasant . . . 168
  398, 514
Mount Pleasant Cumberland
  Presbyterian Church 525
Mountain Mills . . . 530
Mountain Mills Factory
  183, 531
Muscle Shoals 162

Nash Co., NC 512
Nashville, TN 161
  218, 382, 384
Natchez Trace . 163, 164
New Amsterdam 527
New Brunswick 172
New England 216, 504, 535
New Hampshire 504
New Jersey 171
  182, 207, 522
New Orleans, LA . . . 186
  220, 382
New York 171
  182, 210, 509, 521
Newbern 527
Newberry, SC 210
Newburgh 199
Newnan, GA 526
Newsom's Springs 168, 208
Norfolk Co., England 197
Norfolk, VA 192
North Carolina . . . 168
  169, 171, 181, 182, 184
  188, 190, 192, 196, 202
  208, 221, 371, 372, 379
  380, 392, 393, 396, 397

North Carolina . . . 398
  501, 502, 503, 506, 507
  510, 512, 519, 524, 525
  526, 529, 530, 536
Northampton Co., NC . 193
  525

Oaks, The . . . 195, 197
Occoposo 521
Ohio 171
Ohio Medical College 220
Oklahoma City, OK . . 210
Old Bethel 372
Oxfordshire, England 389

Paducah, KY 385
Paris, France 517
Pennsylvania 171
  216, 384, 385, 390, 513
  530, 531
Perryville 526
Pettus Co., MO . . . 398
Philadelphia Medical
  College . . . 385, 524
Philadelphia, PA . . 391
  513, 532
Pickens Co., AL 202, 221
Pickwick Dam, TN . . 165
Pittsylvania Co., VA 391
Pontotoc, MS . 163, 165
Poplar Creek 166
  167, 183, 512, 523
Pride Station . 392, 507
Pulaski, TN 392

Queen's College,
  Cambridge, England 208

Raleigh, NC 371, 392, 507
Ramsey, England . . . 207
Raven Bluff 168
Red Rock 168
Richmond, VA 187
  392, 393
Ricks Avenue 195
Rock Creek . . 165, 169
  215, 216, 218, 219, 501
Rock Creek Church . . 184
  218
Rock Island 392
Rockingham Co., VA . 509
  533
Rockingham, VA . . . 380
Roscoe Community . . 523
Russell Valley 221, 375
Russellville 159
  161, 163, 166, 181, 206
  214, 221, 515, 522, 536
Rutherford Co., TN . 519

St. John's Episcopal
  Church, Tuscumbia . 209
  390
St. Louis Medical College
  394
San Antonio, TX 386, 529
San Diego, CA 213
San Marcos, TX . . . 512

602

INDEX TO PLACES 603

Sand Rock 168
Sardis, MS 212
Schnectady, NY . . . 509
Scotland 172
Sheffield . . . 215, 530
Shelbyville, TN . . . 510
Shirley, VA 375
Smith Creek 166
Smithsonian Institute 165
South Carolina . . . 168
  169, 171, 181, 182, 208
  214, 219
South Florence . . . 168
Spotsylvania Co., VA 392
  525
Spring Creek 166
  221, 392
Spring Valley 164
  176, 182, 201, 514, 516
Springfield, MO . . . 210
Srygley Beat 215
Stage Well 208
Stinking Bear Creek . 166
Stoke Co., NC 398
Stout's Beat 162
Switzerland 376

Tennessee 168
  169, 171, 181, 182, 186
  187, 197, 203, 205, 207
  209, 218, 219, 383, 384
  390, 392, 394, 396, 500
  504, 505, 506, 510, 511
  515, 519, 520, 521, 534
Tennessee Baptist College
  218

Tennessee River . . . 162
  163, 165, 168, 212, 530
Tennessee Valley . . 164
  165, 204, 382
Texas 189
  192, 201, 208, 386, 387
  388, 504, 511, 512, 534
Tharp Springs 206
Throckmorton Co., TX 207
Tishomingo Co., MS . 161
  165
Town Creek 162, 166, 504
Town Creek Triangle . 162
  168, 182, 183, 184, 189
  190, 372, 395, 396, 398
  504, 531
Trinity 188
  189, 190, 525
Trumbull Co., OH . . 199
Tupelo, MS . . . 163, 522
Tuscaloosa . . 161, 527
Tuscaloosa Co., AL . 213
Tuscumbia 160
  163, 168, 169, 170, 179
  182, 183, 184, 185, 186
  187, 192, 194, 197, 199
  200, 201, 203, 204, 205
  206, 207, 208, 209, 210
  211, 212, 213, 214, 215
  220, 269, 371, 373, 374
  375, 376, 378, 379, 380
  382, 383, 384, 385, 386
  388, 389, 390, 391, 392
  399, 400, 501, 503, 504
  506, 507, 508, 509, 511
  513, 514, 515, 516, 517

Tuscumbia . 518, 519, 520
  521, 523, 524, 525, 526
  531, 532, 533, 534, 535

University of Alabama 504
  526

Vermont 504
Vinson Place 505
Virginia 168
  169, 171, 181, 184, 185
  203, 209, 371, 374, 375
  379, 380, 385, 391, 392
  393, 394, 505, 509, 515
  523, 525, 526, 533, 534

Waco, TX . 200, 395, 512
Wake Co., NC 188
  380, 396, 397
Walter Valley, MS . . 523
Warboys, England . . 207
Warren Co., NC . . . 187
Washington Co., AL . 394
Weldon, NC 507
West Point Academy . 513
Wheeler Mountain 206, 500
Williamsburg, VA . . 209
Wilson Place 505
Winston Co., AL . . . 214

Yazoo City, MS 161, 194
Yorks Bluff 168

INDEX TO CEMETERIES

Abernathy Family . . 514
Atkisson Family . . . 530
Bethel 372
Bethlehem 183
Byrd Family 399
Cherokee 532
Eggleston Family . . 374
Fennel Family 189
Foster Family 500
Guy Family 524
Hampton Family . . . 398
King Family 189
LaGrange 189
  193, 195, 392, 393, 394
  395, 397, 523, 528
Leigh Family 504
Madding Family . . . 185
Mayers Family 194
Mhoontown . . . 501, 503
Mt. Pleasant . 372, 398
Oakwood, Sheffield . 388
Oakwood, Tuscumbia . 182
  192, 211, 215, 221, 371
  382, 388, 389, 390, 391
  392, 506, 507, 516, 517
  518, 519, 521, 523, 528
  533
Old Brick 398
Prewitt Family . . . 395
  396, 397
Pride Family 508

INDEX TO NAMES 607

Abernathy 172
  David 514
  Eliza (Wright) . . . 514
  John T. . 170, 513, 514
  John W. . . . 170, 514
  Lavenia 514
  Robert Townes, Dr. . 197
   198, 214, 514
  Sarah (Ellett) . . 514
Adams 172
  Kate 375
Aldridge 172
  Emma L. (Barton) . 532
  Jane B. 534
  Samuel H. . . 532, 534
  Thomas 534
Alexander . . . 172, 398
  Aaron 506
  J. F., Dr. 388
  James W. . . . 170, 525
  John 170
  Mary E. . . . 387, 527
  Mollie 179
  William B. . . 387, 388
Allen 172
  Solomon 171
Allison
  Ann Elizabeth 176, 196
Alsobrook 172
  Alice (Sessum) . . 536
  Bradley . . . 164, 165
  Louis 164, 165
  Martha A. 536
  William B., Col. . 169
   170, 536
Anderson 172
  Isabella 509
Andrews 172
  Eliza 172
  John 172
Armistead 172
  Jennie 178
  Pattie 178
Armstrong . . . 172, 518
  Hiberna 170
  W. H. 529
Ashbridge 376
Askew 173, 503
  Elizabeth N. . . . 503
  Joseph 171
  L. B. 503
Atkisson 172, 203
  Arthur 177, 203
  Caroline H. 177
  Hector . 176, 181, 182
   183, 202, 399, 531
  Hectoria C. 177
  Hester M. 177
  Joel Ann 177
  Lucy (Sherrod) 177, 203
  Martha Jane 177
  Mary M. 177
  Rebecca L. 177
  Sallie (Franklin) . 177
   202, 531
  Sallie W. B. . . . 177
  Susan (Donley) 177, 203
Austill

Austill (cont'd)
  Evan 163
  Jere 163
Austin 172
  Thomas 171
Auten 172
Avery 172
  Betty 179, 212
  Elizabeth F. (Brook) 212
  Fannie E. 388
  Mary E. 387
  Mary Jane 387
  William H., Capt. . 212
   387
Aycock 172
Ayres 172
  George Ann 524

Badgett
  Cordy S. 211
Baisden 172
Baker 172
Baldwin 172
Barbour 394
  Philip Penleton . . 393
  Philip S. 393
  S. B. 393
  Thomas S. 393
Barclay 172, 518
  Anderson, Dr. 506, 528
  Jonathan 506
Barham 221
  Julia A. 202
  Martha A. 180
Barrett 172
  Susan 507
Barton 172, 501
  Amanda . 171, 385, 519
   532, 533, 534
  Annie 385, 510
  Armistead 385, 390, 532
   533, 534
  Arthur 534
  Clark T. 534
  Clark T., Jr. . . . 534
  Elizabeth 534
  Emma L. 532
  Hannah Maria . . . 534
  Hugh, Dr. 534
  Hugh 534
  James Shirley . . . 534
  Jane B. (Aldridge) . 534
  Jane (Harris) . . . 534
  Kate 534
  Lizzie (Petty) . . 534
  Louise Vance . . . 534
  Margaret 519
  Margaret Ann . . . 534
  Mary Shirley . . . 534
  Veto (Clark T., Jr.)
Bates
  J. R. 395
  James 502
  Sallie P. 395
Battle
  Mary 525
Baxter 172
  Ann Carroll . 172, 521

Baxter (cont'd)
  Carroll 521
  John 172, 521
  John 521
  Thomas Emmet . . . 521
Beard 503
Beaumont 172
Beavers
  Martha 168
Beecher
  Henry Ward 218
Bell 172
  Charles, Dr. . . . 177
  Fannie E. 388
  James Porter . . . 388
  Lucy (Stoddard) . . 177
Bendall
  Ollie Virginia . . 159
Bennett 172
  Mary 172
Berry
  Annie H. . . . 176, 192
Bester
  D. P., Dr. . . 189, 190
Bibb
  Thomas, Gov. . . . 374
Bickley 172
Biggs 172
Black 172
  Ellen Lavinia J. . 180
  George 180
Blackburn 172
Blakemore 510
  White 510
Blanton 172
Blocker 172
  Abner B., Col. 206, 392
  Elizabeth 177
  Julia (Plummer) . . 177
   392
  William C. 392
Boles
  H. Leo 218
Borden
  William 536
Bowen 172
  Charles F. . . 177, 206
  Ellen D. (Stoddard) 177
  Mary E. (Devaney) . 206
  Wilkerson C. . . . 206
Bowers
  Mary 509
Bowlin
  William 170
Boyles
  Adah 202
  Mary (Cook) 202
  Polly (Mary Cook)
Braddock 164
Braden 172
  Andrew 511
  Armistead 511
  Barton 511
  Jackson 511
  Jane (Pride) . . . 511
  John 511
  Martha (Petree) . . 511
  Martha (Pope) . . . 511

INDEX TO NAMES 608

Braden (cont'd)
William 511
Bradley 172
Bradshaw 172
John 172
Brady 172
M. B. 172
Brandon
Mattie 178
Bresler 172
Abraham 172
Bronson 186
Catherine P. . . . 186
Brook
Elizabeth F. . . . 212
Brotherton
W. D. . . 369, 526, 536
Brown 172, 503
Eliza Minerva . . 390
Thomas 172
Bryon 172
Buck 172
Burcham 172
Burgess 219
Burns 172
Jeremiah 171
Burton 176, 200
Amelia L. 200
Mary Elizabeth . . 201
Butts
Becky 180
Bynum 172
F. W. 169, 170
Byrd 172
Cicero 399
James 399
Michael C. 399

Cammack
Edward 200
Camp 186, 187
Campbell
Alexander 374
Cannon 172
Agnes 518
John 518
Cantrell 172
Carlock . . . 172, 398
Carloss 172, 501, 509
Archelaus 529
Halcott Pride 529, 530
James A. 369, 529, 536
Laura (Patterson) . 529
Lucy (Grandbury) . 530
Mary 529
Ruth 529
W. J. 530
Carmack 172
James 172
Carmichael
Archie 201
Cornelia 179
Carr 212
Emma 179
Carroll 172
George W. . . 170, 514
Carter . . 172, 211, 398
Burnett 179

Carter (cont'd)
Edward, Dr. . . . 213
F. 390
James 390
Johannah W. . . . 179
Mary Louisa . 179, 211
Parkerson, Dr. . . 179
Cary 172
Cheatham 172
Littleberry . . . 525
Mary B. 525
Chidester 172
Chisholm . . . 172, 211
Obadiah 179
Sarah Jane 179
Christian 179
Annie 185
Elizabeth (Langston)
. . . . . . 175, 185
John Tate 185
Claiburn 172
P. H. 171
Clay 172, 507
Cleveland 376
Clounch 172
Coats
Annie (Delaney) . 216
Benjamin 216
J. P. 216
Sarah Jane 180, 181, 215, 216
Cobb 172
Adline (Ligon) . . 200
Asa 200
Azekiah 170
Mary Frances . . . 200
Robert Ligon . . . 200
Tom 200
Tomithous 200
Coburn 172, 221
Effie (Fort) 181, 221
Ernest . . . 180, 221
Estelle (McCulloch) 180
Frances 181
James 180
Katie (Kirkland) . 180, 221
Katie (Richardson) 181
Lula (Townsend) . 180
Martha A. (Barham) 180, 221
Mary (McCulloch) . 181
Mattie (Hooper) . 180
Maury 181, 221
Neomie (Howard) . 180
Paul . . 163, 165, 180, 221
Percy S. . . 180, 221
Theophilus 180, 181, 182, 184, 221
Theophilus Bester . 181
William T. . 180, 221
Cockburn . . . 173, 521
Elizabeth 170
G. L. 520, 521
Lem (G. L.) . . . .
Theophilus W. . . 520
Cockrill . . . 173, 518

Coffee
A. D., Capt. . . . 175
Camill (Wilmarth) . 175
John, Gen. 175
Colbert
Chief 164
George . 162, 163, 164
James 162, 163
Levi . . 162, 163, 164
Lochland 164
Sophia 164
William . 162, 163, 164, 165
Collum 503
Conner
James 392
Cook 173, 202
Amanda . . . 532, 533
Henry 519, 533
Jane 519
Jane L. 519
Mary 202
Polly (Mary) . . . .
Coons 173
Samuel, Dr. . . . 170
Cooper 173
Anna (Langston) . 177
Anne (Shine) . . . 177
Birt Harrington 179, 210
Charles . . . 185, 210
Edmund 203
Elizabeth (Blocker) 177
Elizabeth H. . . . 179
Elizabeth (Stoddard) 177
Frances H. . . 192, 210
Harriett 179
I. T. 519
James Parks . 177, 179
Jane 177
Jennie P. 179
John William . 177, 205
Julia Frances . . 177
Julia P. (Blocker) 177
Langston 177
Langston M. . 179, 210
Lydal Bacon . 169, 176, 179, 181, 182, 192, 209, 210, 518
Martha 179
Martha (Jackson) . 203, 210
Mattie H. 179
Mattie (Wells) . . 179
Mollie Rufus . . . 177
Patsie (Martha Jackson)
Samuel J., Dr. 179, 210
Sarah Amelia . . . 177
Susan McCulloch 177, 205
Susan (McCulloch) . 177
William 169, 177, 181, 182, 194, 203, 204, 205, 206, 517, 518
William, Dr. . 179, 210
Copeland 173
Reuben 503
Cormack 173
Craig 173, 398
J. F. 369, 536

INDEX TO NAMES

Craig (cont'd)
  Maude 520
Crawford 536
  Ida 199
  James 172
Creamer 173
  G. W. 170
  George W. 171
Creek's 165
Crittenden 173
Croom 173
  Eliza Maria Wren . 174
  Richard, Dr. . . . 184
Cross 173
  Amanda Rebecca . . 527
  Arabella (Prince) . 527
  Benjamin Jesse . . 527
  Jesse 526
  Lyda (Jennings) . . 527
  Mary (Alexander) . 527
  Mary Ann F. (Harris) 527
  Mary L. 526
  William C., Dr. . . 526
  William Cyprian . . 527
Crowell 173
Croxton 173, 214
  B. M., Dr. 214
  Elizabeth Melissia 179
    214
  Ellen 214
  Mary 214
  Narcissa 214
Cummins 189
  A. J. M. 190
  Mary 175
Curry 173
  Mary M. 179
Curtis
  Ann 200, 397
  Burchet 175
  John 191
  Mary 176, 191
  Mary 191
Cushman
  H. B. 162

Dale
  William D. 394
Davidson 173
  Clayton 171
Davis 172
  J. S. 373
  Jefferson 213
  John W. 203
  Samuel 172
Davison 398
Dawson 193
Day 173
Dean 173
  Joseph W., Capt. . 531
    532
DeFour 173
DeGraffenreid 173
  Dolly 186
  Metcalfe 186
Delaware 375
Delony 173
  E. B., Dr. . 170, 369

Delony cont'd
  Edward . . . 170, 189
  Fox, Judge 372
  James, Dr. 512
  Martha Rebecca 175, 189
  Mollie (Horn) . . . 512
  Woodruff . . . 369, 395
Dent 173
Deshler 173
  David . . 171, 172, 390
    391, 513
  James . . 390, 391, 513
Desprez 173, 517
  Susan 517
  William, Dr. . 172, 517
Devaney
  Mary E. 206
Dial 173
Dickson 173
  Barton 532
  Elizabeth B. . . . 534
  W. M. 170
  William 534
Didlake 173
Dill 173
Dillahunty
  Major 168
  Thomas 168
Dillard 173
Dobbs 173
  John E. 177
  Susan 177
Donley 173, 531
  E. J. 399
  Hester M. 177
  John E. . 177, 202, 214
  Susan 177, 531
Donthit 173
Doss 520
Dotson 173
Dougan
  George W. 383
Douthat (Donthit) . .
Downs 173
  William W. 170
Doxey 173
  Samuel H. 400
Drake 212
Duboise 173
Duncan 173
Dunlap
  Hugh, Gen. 383

East 176, 201
  Amelia L. B. . 200, 201
  Thomas 200, 201
Edington
  Martha R. 515
Edwards
  Elizabeth 382
Eggleston 173
  John L. 374
  Polly 375
  Samuel O. 171, 374, 375
  W. F. 374
Elkins 173
Ellett 173
  Deacon Edmund . . . 171

Ellett (cont'd)
  John 514
  Mary (Miller) . . . 178
  Sarah 514
Elliott 173, 188
  Elizabeth P. . . . 175
  Isabella . . . 172, 391
  James 391
  Robert 170
  Samuel 175, 187
Enlow
  Calvin 515
Erwin 387
  W. G. 388
Ethridge
  Jack 168
Evans 173
Eve 175, 187, 188
  Anne P. 175
Eves (Eve) . . . . .
Farley 173
Felton 173, 191, 510
  Ann Eliza 393
  Elizabeth . . 393, 510
  H. K. 393
  Hilliard . . . 510, 511
  J. B. 393, 510
  J. E. 183
  Martha Ann 510
  Thadeus 170, 175, 190
    510, 511
Fennel 191
  James 175, 190
  Mary 189
  Mary Curtis (King) 175
    190
Field
  Eugene 389
Fielder 173
Fields 196
Finley 173, 213
Finney
  Michael 206
Foote
  Henry S. 521
*Fort 173, 221
  Charlotte (Bryant) 176
    192
  Effie . . . 181, 221
  Munroe S. . 192, 193
  Olivia 192
Foster 173, 501
  Elizabeth M. . . . 500
  George 501
  Josiah 500
  Richard 501
  Sallie E. 500
Fowler 173
  Silas M. 393
Franklin
  Benjamin 202
  Sallie . 177, 202, 531
Frye 380, 532

Gadd 173
Galbraith 173
  Ellen S. 373

INDEX TO NAMES 610

Gannaway
  Mary 176, 197, 199, 201
Gargis 173
  Henry 183
  Nancy 178
Garner 173
  A. 170
  Hectoria C. 177
  Milton 203
  Robert Milton 177, 203
  Sallie 203
Garrett 173
  Lewis 170
  Mary 179, 212
Gassaway 173
Gee
  Mary 192
Geise 173, 385
  George 171, 384, 385
  Henry 384
  Martha Ann 384
  Reuben 385
Gibbs 173
  Thomas 171
Gilbert 173
Giles 378
Gill 173
Gillean 173, 398
Gilmore
  Frank T., Jr. . . . 530
Gipson 173
Gledall 173
  B. 172, 392
Godley 374
  Philip G. 171
Goins 173
Goodloe . . 173, 501, 520
  Albert G. 380
  David Short . 379, 380
  J. C. 169, 170
  J. Calvin 380
  Julia T. .178, 207, 380
  Mary (Lane) 380
  Paul 380
  Robert, Capt. . . . 379
  Robert Atlas 170, 178
    378, 379, 380
  Sarah Louise . . . 380
Goodwin . . 173, 189, 190
  Ann 189
  Edward, Prof. . . . 175
  John 177, 190
  Sarah Amelia (Cooper)177
Gorman 173
  Edward 172
  James 172
Grandbury
  Lucy 530
Gray
  Elizabeth F. . . . 389
  Martha W. 389
  Robert H. 389
  Young A., Dr. . . . 389
Green 173
  Isabella G. 177
  John N. 515
Greenhill 173
Gregg 510

Gregg (Cont'd)
  James 187
  John 187
  Mollie (Garth) . . 187
  Nathan 187
  Nathan, Jr. 187
Gregory
  Anna 179
Grissom . . 173, 180, 221
Guernsey
  Duane 178
Gurley 173
  Davis 170, 512
Guy 173, 371
  Elizabeth N. . . . 178
  Esther J. 524
  Esther (Sharp) . . 524
  I. P. . 178, 208, 525
  Joseph, Dr. 524
  Joseph Albert 170, 524
    525
  Lorenzo 524
  Martin 524
  Mattie 378, 524, 525
    536

Hailey
  James T. 170
Hall 398
  Ernest 536
  G. D. 388
  William 523
Halsey 173, 505, 506
  James 505
  Mattie 179
Hampton 173
  Cynthia 398
  Cynthia Amanda . . 398
  M. B. . . 169, 170, 398
  Manoah Bostic . 162, 398
Hanks 173
Hardeman
  N. B. 218, 219
Hardy 173, 393, 527
  James M. 392
  Thomas 190
Haris
  Manerva 171
Harrington 173
  Birt 176, 179, 182, 184
    192, 210
  Eliza Jane 392
  Frances 176, 179, 192
    210
  Harriet Adelia (Jarman)
    192
  Harriet C. (Johnston)
    176, 179, 210
  Samuel J. . . 176, 192
  William H. 392
Harris 173, 187
  Charlotte (Ricks) . 192
  Ida W. 179, 213
  Jane 534
  John 192
  Martha 170
  Mary Ann Frances . 527
  Willie 179, 213

Harrison 398
Hart 173
  Joseph 172
  Lewis 172
Hawkins 534
  J. S., Prof. . 185, 393
Helms 518
Henderson 173
  Anna J. 172
  George S. 172
  Hugh 178
  Jennie T. 178
Hennigan
  Stewart 168
  Henry 173
Hester 214
  Ellen (Croxton) . . 214
Hicks 173
Higdon
  Jane L. L. . . 172, 373
  Z. Taylor . . 172, 373
Higgins
  James W. 171
Hill
  Andrew
    Chestena Arkansas S. 180
  Dora J. S. . . 180, 219
  John 184
  R. A. 180
Hillman 173
  Joseph 172
Hindman 173, 385
  Samuel 171
Hinton
  George H. 188
Hobgood 173, 535
  Elijah . 169, 170, 536
  John 169, 170, 535, 536
  Martha A. (Alsobrook)
    536
  Virginia M. . 393, 535
Hocutt 202
Hodges
  Fleming 396
Hodgkins 173, 390
  Frederick D. 172, 389
    390
Hogan 221
Hogun 173, 526
  Elizabeth 179
  James H. 170
  John 169, 170
  Sarah C. 384
Holesapple 173
  J. C. 178, 208
  Lallie Virginia N. 178
  W. C. 532
Holley 173
Hooks . . 173, 389, 398
  Catherine (Kenan) . 194
  Curtis 388
Hooper 221
  Frances C. 181
  John 181
  Mattie 180
Hopkins 204
  M. A. 530
Horn 173, 511

INDEX TO NAMES 611

Horn (cont'd).
  Josiah 167, 512, 523
  Mollie 512
Hornsbey . . . .
Hornsby 173
Houston 386
  James 386
  N. J., Dr. 386
Hubbard
  Mary 180
Hudson 173
Hughes 398
Hunt 173
  Mollie H. 512
  W. H., Capt. 512
Hunter 173
Huston 173, 518
  Annie (Barton) . 385, 510
  James M., Dr. . . 385, 510
  Nathaniel, Dr. . . . 170
  Sudie 510
Hyde 173, 507

Inman 173
  John D. 206, 519
Isbell 173

Jackson . . . 163, 173, 521
  James 171
  Martha 203
  W. M. 383
  William 170
Jarman 173
  Amos . . 162, 170, 371, 372
  H. 372
  Harriett Adelia 176, 192
  Louisa Ann 372
  Mary 372, 372
James 173, 503
  Aaron A. 159
  Ollie Virginia B. . 159
  R. L. . . 159, 163, 500
Jefferson
  Thomas 165
Jeffreys 173
Jenkins 173
  Thomas B. 171
Jennings
  Lyda 527
Jinx 173
Johnson
  Dick, Maj. 392
  J. E. 392
  Jacob, Dr. . . 169, 170
  John 168
  Kate B. 534
  W. A., Col. . . 159, 215
    534
Johnston
  Harriett C. . . 176, 179
    210
Jones 173, 188
  Burchet Felton . . 189
  Camilla (Wilmarth) 175
    186
  Catherine B. . . . 516
  James T., Dr. . 175, 186

Jones (cont'd) . . . . .
  John Curtis, Dr. . . 190
  Martha (Burchet) . . 393
  Susan (King) . 175, 189
    190
  Tignal . . . 170, 175, 183
    189, 190, 393
  Vincler 168
Julian 173
  Archie 213
  Charley Minta . . . 180
  Elizabeth Melissia
    (Croxton) . 179, 214
  Ellen Lavinia . . . 180
  Frank Newsum . 180, 215
  Henrie Scott . . . 180
  Mary (McReynolds) . 180
  Milton Croxton . . 180
  Owen Nelson . 180, 215
  William Croxton 180, 215
  William Reese 179, 181
    182, 199, 213, 214, 215
    519
Kahl 173
  John 171
  Malinda 173
Kalm
  Peter 166
Karg 173, 398
Keaghy 173
  Samuel 172
Keenon
  Calphurnia C. . . . 389
Keenum 173
Keeton 173
Keller . . . 173, 376, 518
  Arthur Henley 195, 198
    199, 209, 210, 213, 214
    375, 376, 381, 508, 509
    517, 519, 522, 523, 529
    530, 531
  Casper 376
  David 375, 376
  Helen . . 167, 375, 376
  Kate (Adams) . . . 375
  Mary F. 375
Kennedy 380
  Sarah Louise G. . . 380
Kennerly 173, 505
  Charlotte 505
  James 505, 528
  Kate 505
  Rebecca F. 528
Kent 173
Kilburn 173
Kimbrough 173
  S. E. 501
  W. B. 531
King . . . 163, 173, 191
  Ann Lafayette . . . 175
  Ann Lafayette 175, 190
  Burchet Curtis 170, 175
    189, 190
  Eliza Jane . 175, 189
  Frank 165
  Hartwell .162, 169, 175
    181, 182, 183, 188, 189

Hartwell (Cont'd)
  190, 191, 397, 510
  Hartwell, Jr. . 170, 175
  Margaret (Pick) . . 175
  Martha (Burchet) . 175
  Martha Rebecca (Delony)
    175, 189
  Mary (Cummins) . . 175
  Mary (Curtis) 175, 190
  Mary Henderson (Smith)
    175
  Oswald . . 169, 170, 175
    189
  Paul 170, 175, 189, 190
  Philemon . . 175, 189
  Richard 188
  Robert . 169, 170, 175
    189
  Susan 175
  Washington Lafayette 175
Kirk
  Mary Wallace . . . 188
Kirkland 221
  Katie . . . 180, 221
Kulland
  John 170
Kumpe 173
  Catherine F. . . . 528
  George E., Dr. 172, 393
    505, 527, 528
  Rebecca F. 528

Lancaster 173
Landers 173
Lane . . . 173, 501, 509
  Isaac . . 169, 170, 380
  Mary 380
Larimore
  Theophilus Brown . 218
Laster 536
Lavinder 521
Lawrence
  Lucinda 177
  Mary 526
Lawson
  Jack, Capt. 385
Leckey 173
  Alexander . . 172, 373
  Ellen S. (Galbraith) 373
  Hugh C. . . . 172, 373
  Jane 172, 373
  Thomas 373
Lee
  Robert E. 375
LeFlore
  Greenwood 203
Leftwich . 168, 210, 371
  388, 517, 522
Leggett 173
  G. W. 373
  Irene (Ricks) . . . 194
  Jane (Leckey) . . . 373
  Samuel J. 373
Leigh 173
Letsinger . . . 173, 398
Lewis 383
Lightfoot 373
Ligon . 173, 197, 198, 204

INDEX TO NAMES

Ligon (cont'd)
  Abner W.   176, 197, 199
    210
  Adline 176, 200
  Amelia 176, 200
  Ida (Crawford) 176, 199
    200
  James W.   176, 181, 182
    197, 198, 199, 200, 201
    202
  Julia A. (Barham) . 202
  Mary (Gannaway) 176, 197
    199, 200, 201
  Mary (Boyles) . . . 202
  Mollie 178
  Nancy 176, 200
  P. H. 202
  Polly (Mary Boyles)
  Rebecca E. (Smith)   176
    199
  Thomas Henry . . . 202
  William 201
  Williams 176
Lile
  Amanda Rebecca C. . 527
  Thomas 527
Limerick 173
Lindsay 173
  David Ross 172
  Maud 516
  Robert Burns, Gov. 159
    172, 516
Lindsey 173
*Little 523
Littlepage 512
  Mollie H. 512
Long 173
  James 171
Looney 173
  H. P. 393
Lueddeman 173
Lutch
  Naomi S. 505

Madding
  Camilla (Wilmarth) 175
    186
  Edwin Price 175
  Elisha   162, 170, 174
    181, 182, 184, 185
  Eliza Jane 175, 185, 189
  Eliza Maris Wren (Croom)
    174, 181, 185
  Elizabeth Langston
    (Christian)   175, 185
  Isaac Groom   175, 184
    185
  James Allen   175, 185
  Mary Ann 175, 185
  Richard Thomas 175, 184
  Robert Franklin . . 175
    184, 185
Maddox
  A. J. 387
Malone . . 173, 382, 501
  Addison 515
  Alexander 170, 380, 382
  Eliza Minerva (Brown)390

Malone (cont'd)
  Elizabeth . . 380, 382
  Goodloe Warren 169, 170
    382
  John Lewis . . 169, 170
    390
  Mitchell 382
  Robert B. 390
  Robert G. 388
  Sandy (Alexander)
  W. A. 536
  William 369
Mann 173
  Richard 170
Marlowe
  Christopher 207
Martin
  Nancy 199
Matlock 173
Matthews 173, 522
  Alfred C. . . 522, 523
  Solomon 523
Mattingly 518
  Catherine W. . . . 391
  Thomas 391
Mayers 173
  George W. 193
  James J. 194
  Pheribee (Ricks) . 193
    194
Mayfield
  Lafayette 183
Mays
  Drury 171
McAfee 173
McCaig 173
McClain 173
McCleskey 173
  Alfred 523
  Mary 178
  S. W. L. 523
McClung 173, 204, 506
  Alexander (Col.) . 213
  James Y. 389
  John A. 389
  Susan 389
McCorkle 173
McCormack . . . 173, 395
  F. W. 167, 523
  William . . . 172, 523
McCulloch 221
  Elijah 221
  Estelle 180
  Mary 180
  Susan 177, 221
McDaniel 173
McDonald 173
  James, Col. 171
McGregor
  A. A., Prof.   179, 188
    210, 394, 505, 510, 514
    527
  Harriet C. 179
McKee 173
McKiernan . . . 173, 383
  Bernard . 170, 172, 382
  Charles B., Major . 382
    383

McKiernan (cont'd)
  Mary A. 382
McKinney 173
McReynolds 173, 211, 221
  Lucy B. 179
  Mary 180
Mearers (Mayers)
Meredith 173
  Louisa 526
Merrill 173
Messenger 173
  Asa 171, 213
Meyers (Mayers)
Mhoon 173, 501
  James   169, 170, 380
    502
  James E. 501
  James George . . . 501
  John 502
  Josiah 502
  Letitia (Cotten) . 501
  Lucinda W. 501
  Mary (Goodloe) 380, 501
    502, 503
  Mourning 503
  William Spivey 501, 502
Miller 173
  J. S. 392
  R. R., Capt. . . . 392
  Sally 180
  Susan Adelaide . . 535
Mills 173
Millwater
  Mary Eliza 394
Milner 173
Minott
  Sarah 504
Mitchell 173
  Margaret (Fowler)   389
Mohr
  Charles 505
Monroe 521
Moody 173, 211
  Dan 179
  Elizabeth Frances W. 179
Moore 173, 188
  Annie Lee . . . 180, 220
  Ella Burns . . 180, 220
  John 393
  Joshua Burns   175, 180
    181, 182, 187, 219
  Laura L. 393
  Moses 219
  Nina 180, 220
  Rebecca L. 177
  Robert P. . . 177, 203
  Sallie, Aunt . . . 220
  Susie Erle . . 180, 220
  Thomas Ella   175, 180
    181, 220
  William . . . 219, 220
Moran 173
Morgan
  John T. 170
Moron
  Frank 172
Morrow 398
Morton 173

INDEX TO NAMES 613

Morton (cont'd)
  John 171
Moule 173
Mullens 173, 524
  Nancy 199
Murdoch 173
  James 172
Murdock
Murphy
  Mariah 171
Myatt 173, 191
  Aldridge 191, 200, 395
    396, 397
  Ann (Curtis) . 200, 397
Myhan 173

Nail 173
Napier 173
  John S., Dr. 176, 200
    395, 397
  Mary C. 395
  Nancy L. S. 200
Neal .
  William M. 172
Neals 173
Neely 173
Nelson 173
  Fannie 178
  Frederick B., Judge 205
  Mollie N. 178
  Owen O. 205
  R. D. 178
  Susan McC. (Cooper) 177
    205
  William A. . . 177, 205
Newlett 214
  Mary (Croxton) . . 214
  Narcissa (Croxton) 214
Newnum
  Annie 178
Newsom 173
  Charles E. . . 178, 208
  Edward H. 178, 182, 183
    208, 518, 520, 525
  Elizabeth 178
  Fannie 178
  John E. 178, 208
  Lallie Virginia . . 178
  Mary Ann W. 178
  Mattie B. 178
  Millard . . . 178, 208
  Mollie 178
  Mollie L. 178
  Penelope R. 178, 208
    520
  Whit 178
  William B. 178
Newsum 173, 209
  Alexander 209
  B. F., Dr. . . 209, 518
  William H., Dr. 209, 517
  William O. 209
Nichols 173
Noland 179, 211
Nooe . . . 173, 204, 518
  John A. 526
  Virginia 526
Nool (Nooe)

Norman 173, 518
  Felix Grundy . . . 519
  Jane L. (Cook) . . 519

Oates (Oats
Oats 173
  Samuel K. 170
O'Conner 173
  Dennis 172
Oden
  Susan 180
Ohlman 173
  Peter 172
Old 173
  Elizabeth 531
Oliver 173
Oolisk 206
Osborn 173
Ottaway 173
  Elizabeth G. (Kidd) 392
Overcash 173
Owens
  Thomas M., Dr. 193, 212
    214, 378

Page
  Ellen V. . . . 179, 211
Paine 173
  Amanda Malvina 393, 394
  Bishop . 393, 507, 527
  Mary Eliza M. . . . 394
  Robert 394
Palmer 173
  Ann E. 509
  Charles 171
  Charles B. 509
  Charles R., Dr. . . 386
    509
  Isabella (Anderson) 509
  Mary (Bowers) 509, 510
  Philip 171, 509, 510
  Sudie (Huston) . . 510
Parbury
  William, Dr. . . . 396
Parham 521
  William 520
Parkhill
  Ella 180
Parrish
  Nicholas 171
Patterson 173
  Ida 176, 199
  James A. . 170, 171, 199
  Laura 529
  Nancy M. 199
Patton 173, 503
  N. W. 503
Payne 173
Pearsall 173
  Anne 175
  Catherine . . 175, 186
  Dolly 186
  Edmond 181
  Edward   170, 175, 182
    186, 187, 188, 220
  Edward, Jr. . 175, 188
  Elizabeth 175
  James M. 186

Pearsall (cont'd)
  Jeremiah 186
  Letitia 188
  Nathan . . . 175, 188
  Parthenia (Shearan) 175
    187, 188
  Sarah Letitia . . . 175
  Thomas Ella . 175, 181
Peden 173
  Warren 170
Penick 173
  Edward 171
Person 173
  Helen T. 178
  John 178
  William R. 171
Peters 173
  Charles 504
  John 504
  Lemuel 504
  Naomi S. (Lutch) . 505
  Samuel 504
  Sarah (Minott) . . 504
  Thomas M. . . 504, 505
Petree
  Martha 511
Pettit
  James T. 177
  Jane (Cooper) . . . 177
  Jennie 179
Petty
  Lizzie 534
Phagan
  W. J. 183
Phillips 173
Pick
  Margaret 175
Pierce 192
  Charlotte 192
Piller 173
Plummer
  Julia 177
Poe
  Edgar Allen 532
Polk
  James K. 505
Polhemus
  Margaret 178
Pollock 173
  John 171
Pope 173
  Martha 511
  Sallie 176, 197
Porter 173
Porterfield 173
Potts 173
Pounders 173
Powell 173
Powers 173
  David 172
Preuit (Prewit)
Prewit 173
  Richard 162, 170, 395
    396
Price 173, 534
Pride . . 173, 501, 520
  Edward, Major 508, 509
    529

INDEX TO NAMES 614

Pride (cont'd)
  Eliza M. 509
  H. J.   169, 171, 509
  Hock (H. J.)
  J. P., Dr. 508
  Jack (John F.)
  Jane 511
  John Fletcher 169, 170
    392, 507, 508, 529
  Nathaniel 169, 170, 509
  Ruth 529
  Thomas 509
  William 171
Prince 173
  Arabella 527
  Sidney Smith, Dr. . 393
Prout 173
  H. W. 171
Pybas 173, 507
  Anna 507
  Benjamin 506

Quillen 173
Quillin 173

Ragland 174
  George D. 171
  Samuel 171
Rand 174, 191
  Catherine 175
  John, Dr. 170, 175, 187
    191, 397
  Mosley Ann . . 176, 192
Rather . . 174, 188, 205
  Bessie 205
  Eldon R. 177
  John D. . 175, 187, 220
  Julia Frances (Cooper)
    177
  Letitia 188
  Sarah Letitia . . . 175
Rauhoff 174
Redwine 174
Reed 211
  Susan 179
Reese 213
Reilly
  Eliza Jane 392
  James F. 392
  Susan E. 392
Reynolds 174
Rhea 174
Rice
  Ebenezer 197
Richards 174
Richardson . . . 174, 221
  Dall 515
  Henry 515
  Katie 181
  Louisa W. 515
  Martha R. E. . . . 515
  Robert McGary . . . 515
Rickard 174
Ricks 174, 195, 197, 393
  Abe, Dr. 193, 194, 197
  Abraham 169, 170, 176
    181, 182, 192, 193, 194
    195, 196, 392

Ricks (cont's)
  Abram 176, 197
  Ann Elizabeth (Allison)
    176
  Benjamin Sherrod . 193
    194
  Birdie 197
  Charlotte 192
  Charlotte Bryant (Fort)
    176, 192, 196
  Eliza (Toney) . . 193
  Elizabeth 193
  Fannie (Winter) . 193
  Isaac 192
  Isaac, (Jr.) . . . 192
  John 194
  John Sherrod . . . 193
  Lillian 197
  Martha 192
  Mary (Gee) 192
  Mary M. . . . 192, 193
  Olivia (Fort) . . 192
  Orrin 192
  Patsie (Martha)
  Pheribee . . 193, 194
  Richard Henry 176, 192
    196
  Robert 193
  Sallie (Pope) 176, 197
  William F. . 176, 196
Ritter 174
  George 171
Roberts 174
  James 170
Robertson
  Felix, Dr. 382
Robinson 174
Rogers 174
Rollston 174
Rosenthal 174
  B. 172
  H. 172
Ross 174, 520
  Alexander 392
  Elizabeth 392
  F. A. 384
  Richard L. 179
Roundall 174
Rowland 174
  T. T. 172
  W. T. 519
Russell 174
  Mary Elizabeth Barton
    (Sugg) 201
  William, Major . . 221
Russey 206
Rutherford 174
  George 171
  Friend 171
Rutland 501
  Hannah Marria 520, 534
  James 520
  John Armistead . . 520
  John W. . 519, 520, 534
  Joseph J. 520
  Margaret Ann . . . 534
  Penelope 178, 208, 520
  Sarah (Goodloe) . . 380

Rutland (cont'd)
  Turner, Dr. . . . 520
  Watt 380
  Wells 378, 520
  Whitman . . . 170, 520

Sadler 174
Saltzer 174
Sample 174
Sampson 174
Samuel
  Agnes 207
  Alice 207
  John 207
Sanderson 174
Sandlin
  Ann 180
Sargent
  Susan 221
  Temple 221
Saunders
  Claborne 521
  James E., Col. 168, 184
    185, 186, 187, 189, 190
    216, 376, 395, 504, 505
    526
  Turner 394
Sawtelle 174
  B. N., Rev. . . . 370
Scobey
  Jennie 180
Scott 174, 214
  J. W. 172
  Winfield, Gen. . . 214
Scruggs 520, 534
  Emma . . 369, 532, 536
Sessum
  Alice 536
Sevier 174
Sewell 525
Shackleford
  Joseph 518
Shaller
  John M., Dr. . 180, 220
  Susie Erle (Moore) 180
Sharp
  Esther 524
Shaw 394
  Amanda Malvina . . 394
Shearan
  Parthenia 175
Shearon . . . . . .
Sheffield 174
  Joe 400
  Patrick H. 399
Shegag 174
Sherrod 174, 175
  Ann 170
  Lucy 177, 203
Shigley (Srygley)
Shine 174, 205
  Anna 177
  John G. 169, 170, 205
    206, 516
Shirley
  Mary 534
Short
  Sarah 379

INDEX TO NAMES 615

Shrygley (Srygley)
Simpson 174
  James 163
  Lula (Merrill) . . 534
Skidmore 174
  Nancy (Ligon) . . 200
  Thomas . . . 176, 200
Sledge
  Alexander, Dr. . . 169
  Joshua 170
  Macklin . . . 169, 170
Sloan 174
Smith 185
  B. J. 377, 524
  E. S. 377
  Esther J. 524
  James . . . 184, 199
  Jeff "Uncle" . . . 215
  Laura Frances . . . 377
  Mary (Henderson) . 175
  Nancy (Millens) . . 199
  Rebecca E. . . 176, 199
Southall 174
*Spangler 174
  Daniel 512
Spencer 174
Spivey
  Alice 502
  Jemima 502, 503
  Joshua 502
  Moses 502, 503
Spottswood 375
Srygley . . . 174, 218
  Ann (Sandlin) . . . 180
  Ann (Wallace) . . . 216
  Becky (Butts) . . . 180
  Birdie 216
  Chestena Arkansas . 180
  Dona Ann Marth Minerva
    Constance Louisa Jane
    180
  Dora J. . . . 180, 219
  Ella (Parkhill) . . 180
  Felix Grundy . 180, 219
  Fernando Wallace . . 180
    219
  Filo Bunyan . 180, 219
  Fletcher Douglass . 169
    180, 216, 218, 219, 501
  Floyd Lamar . 180, 219
  George 216
  James H. 180, 181, 184
    215, 216, 218, 219
  Jennie (Scobey) . . 180
  Laude 180
  Mary (Hubbard) . . 180
  Sally (Miller) . . 180
  Sarah Jane (Coats) . 180
    181, 215, 219
  Susan (Oden) . . . 180
Stafford 174
Stanley 174
  Jemima 502
  Jonathan 502
  Mary 502
Stebbens 174
Steele 174
  John A., Judge 203, 214
    516

Steger 174
  Martha Ann 384
Stein 174
  Charles 172
Stephens 174
  Ann 172
  Hugh 172, 392
Stephenson . . . 174, 180
  Alice . . . 395, 397
  John Calvin . 167, 191
    200, 395, 510, 511, 512
    528
  Mary C. 395
Stevenson
  Jonathan B. . . . 377
Stickles
  J. H., Capt. . 530, 531
  Elizabeth (Old) . . 531
Sticknay 193
*   Elizabeth 193
Stubbs 520
Sturch 174
Sugg 174, 201
  Mary Elizabeth (Burton)
    201
  Thomas H. 201
Sutherland 174
  John 391
Swain 393, 510
  Elizabeth 393

Tackett
  Celia 183
  Coffee 183
  Ellenar C. . . 178, 181
  Sugar 183
Talmadge
  DeWitt 218
Tapp 174
Tartt 174
  Patience A. W. . . 392
  Thomas E. 392
Taylor 174
  Ann 172
  John 172
Teas 174
Tharp 174
Thatcher 174
  Elizabeth E. . . . 382
  Isaiah 382
  Return 382
  Thomas 174
Thompson . . . 174, 508
  Lawrence 170
Thorn 174
Thornton 174
  Lewis Bedford 374, 525
  Louisa (Meredith) . 526
  Virginia (Nooe) . . 526
Throckmorton 174
  Agnes 207
  Annie N. 178
  Craig . . . 178, 207
  Edmund E. . . 178, 207
  Helen 178
  James . 171, 178, 181
    182, 183, 206, 207
  Jennie 178
  Jennie A. 178

Throckmortoh (cont'd)
  Julia . . . 178, 207
  Mamie 178
  Margaret . . . 171, 178
  Mary McC. 178
  Mary Miller (Ellett) 178
  Pattie A. W. . . . 178
  Robert 207
  Thomas C. . . 178, 207
Tickle 174
Tompkins 174
  John 509
  Pride 509
Toney 174
  C. A. 175
  Charles Augustus . 175
  Eliza 193
  Mary Ann (Madding) 175
Townes 204, 518
  E. D. 170
  John L. 375
  Polly S. . . . 170, 375
Townsend 221
  Claiborne S., Dr. . 221
  Lula 180
Trabue 174
Trotter 174, 506
Trowbridge 174
  Thomas 171
Truelove 174
Tubb 174
  Jack 222
  James . . . 181, 221
  Joel 221
  Martha (Johnson) . 221
  Martin Erles . . . 221
Tubbaville 174
Tubbs (Tubb)
Tuomey
  Michael 197
Turner 174
  A. J. 171
  Alice W. . . 179, 212
  Charles F. . . 179, 212
  William Milam . . . 212
Tutwiler 174, 186, 527

Underwood 174
Ural 211

Vandiver 174
Van Eaton
  Frank 200
  Tomithous (Cobb) . 200
Vinson 174, 191
  Annie H. (Berry) . 192
  Drury . 169, 170, 175
    181, 182, 191, 397, 505
  Edwin 515
  Fletcher Curtis, Col.
    176, 191
  John 176, 191
  Martha Ann . . 176, 191
  Mary (Curtis) 176, 191
  Mosley Ann (Rand) . 192

Waddell 174
Wadsworth 174
  Ann Eliza 393

INDEX TO NAMES

Wadsworth (cont'd)
  Edward, Dr.   393, 510
    527
Wagnon 174
Walker . . . 174, 204
  Eliza H. 391
  Isaac 171
  Peter 391
Wall 174, 178
  A. C. 178
  Lacy 178
  Mamie T. 178
Wallace
  Ann 216
Wallis
  Dona Ann Martha Minerva
    Constance Louisa Jane
    S. 180
  John 180
Wanner 174
Warren 174
  Henry 393
  Horace 534
  Louise Vance . . . 534
  Robert 170, 172
  William 172
Washington
  Martha Custis . . . 210
Waters
  David C. 384
  John, Dr. 382
  Mary (Anthony) . . 382
Weeden 394
Wells
  Mattie 179
Wheeler . . . 174, 378
  Laura Frances . . . 377
  Lou (Laura Frances)
  W. C., Dr. . . 377, 378
    524, 532
White 174
  John S., Capt. . . 214
  Nancy E. 388
  Robert W. 170
Whitley 174
  Tilmon A. 203
Whitlock 174
  Charley M. . . 178, 183
  Ellenar C. (Tackett) 178
  John 183
  Nancy G. 178
  Nathaniel 178, 181, 183
Whittemore 507
Wilbourn (Wilburn)
Wilburn 174
  Pattie A. 178
Wiley
  Hattie C. (Stoddard) 177
  W. M. 177
Williams 174
  Alice . . . 179, 212
  Anna G. 179
  Betty A. . . 179, 212
  Charles W., Dr. . . 172
    212, 388
  Charley F., Dr. . . 179
  Cornelia C. 179
  Emma C. 179

Williams (cont'd)
  Gideon 504
  Henry 179, 212
  Ida 179
  James William 179, 212
  Mary G. . . . 179, 212
  Mollie A. 179
  O. H. Perry . 179, 181
    182, 183, 212, 387
  Susan Adelaide 392, 535
  T. Wesley . . 179, 212
  Virginia 535
  William G., Prof. . 171
    392, 535
Willis 213
  Andrew Jackson . . 515
Wilson 174, 511
  Belle 510
  Martha Ann (Felton) 510
  Mary Ann 510
  Samuel 171
  Thomas Bell 510
Wingo 174, 398
  Louisa 515
Winstead 174
Winston 174, 516
  Anthony . . . 169, 516
  Catherine B. . . . 516
  E. C. 214
  Edmund S. 521
  Isaac 170, 516
  John Anthony . . . 516
  Stephen 171
  William 170
*Winter 174, 205
  Benjamin R. . 177, 194
  Fannie 193, 194
  Mollie R. (Cooper) 194
  William H. 194
Witt 174
Womble 174, 199
  Charles A., Judge 179
    181, 184, 210, 211, 212
  Charles Adolphus . 179
    212
  Dayton Grave . . . 179
  Elizabeth Frances . 179
  Ellen V. (Page) . 179
    211
  Isaac Newton . 179, 211
    212
  James Alexander . . 179
    211
  Johannah 179
  John Leman 179
  Lucy B. (McReynolds) 179
  Martha Mildred . . 179
  Mary Louisa 179
  Mary M. C. 179
  Sarah Jane 179
  Susan (Reed) . . . 179
  William Amos 179, 211
Wood
  Lewis 392
  Mary Ann 392
  William B. 370
Woodford
  Fannie N. 178

Woodford (cont'd)
  Mary Anna 178
  William 178
Wright 174
  Eliza 514
Wythe
  John Allen 208
Yarbrough 174
  Elizabeth Mary . . 500
  Reuben 501
Yoconi 174
Young 174
  Andrew V. 371
  George E. 370
  Isaac E. 369, 370, 371
    524
  James 392
  Priscilla 371

*Fort, Mary M. Ricks . 192

*Linnaeus 166

*Spangler
  D. L. 524
  Daniel 167, 393, 523
    524
  George Ann (Ayers) 524
  James H. 524

*Stoddard . . . 174, 205
  Ellen D. . . . 177, 206
  Elizabeth 177
  Hattie C. 177
  Isabella G. (Green) 177
  James A. 171, 181, 182
    206
  Lizzie 177
  Lucinda 171
  Lucy 177

*Winter, Catherine
  (Washington) . . . 194

www.ingramcontent.com/pod-product-compliance
Lightning Source LLC
LaVergne TN
LVHW091551060526
838200LV00036B/796